Robert Gray was born in 1945; he grew up and went to school in a country town on the north coast of New South Wales. He trained there as a journalist, and since then has worked in Sydney as an editor, advertising copywriter, reviewer, and buyer for bookshops. His first book of poems, *Creekwater Journal*, was published in 1973, and his most recent, *Lineations*, in 1996. He has been a writer-in-residence at Meiji University in Tokyo and at several universities in Australia, and has won the Adelaide Arts Festival and the New South Wales and Victorian Premiers' Awards for poetry. In 1990 he received the Patrick White Award. With Geoffrey Lehmann he edited two anthologies, *The Younger Australian Poets* and *Australian Poetry in the Twentieth Century*, and he is the editor of *Selected Poems* by Shaw Neilson, and *Drawn from Life*, the journals of the painter John Olsen.

GW00384955

NEW SELECTED POEMS

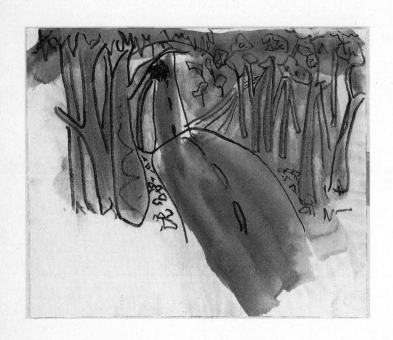

New Selected Poems

Robert Gray

Duffy & Snellgrove
Sydney

First published by Duffy & Snellgrove in 1998
Second edition 1998
PO Box 177 Potts Point, N.S.W. 2011 Australia

Earlier editions of this book were published by
Angus and Robertson and William Heinemann Australia
in 1985, 1990 (twice), 1994 and 1995.

Frontispiece: 'The Narrow Road to
the Deep North' (watercolour).
Endpiece: 'Gum Tree Branches' (pen and ink).
Both are by the author.

The cover, by Alex Snellgrove, incorporates the
author's handwriting. The photo is by Peter Solness.
Typeset in Centaur by Maggie Cooper
Printed by Griffin Press

ISBN 1 875989 23 4

To Dee Jones

Author's Note

In collecting these poems, I would like to acknowledge
the Literature Board of the Australia Council for the fellowships
which have helped in writing many of them.

CONTENTS

Grass Script (1978)

The Skylight (1983)

Piano (1988)

Certain Things (1993)

Lineations (1996)

Creekwater Journal

Journey: the North Coast

Next thing, I wake up in a swaying bunk,
as though on board a clipper
lying in the sea,
and it's the train, that booms and cracks,
it tears the wind apart.
Now the man's gone
who had the bunk below me. I swing out,
cover his bed and rattle up the sash —
there's sunlight rotating
off the drab carpet. And the water sways
solidly in its silver basin, so cold
it joins together through my hand.
I see from where I'm bent
one of those bright crockery days
that belong to so much I remember.
The train's shadow, like a bird's,
flees on the blue and silver paddocks,
over fences that look split from stone,
and banks of fern,
a red clay bank, full of roots,
over a dark creek, with logs and leaves suspended,
and blackened tree trunks.
Down these slopes move, as a nude descends a staircase,
slender white gum trees,
and now the country bursts open on the sea —
across a calico beach, unfurling;
strewn with flakes of light
that make the whole compartment whirl.
Shuttering shadows. I rise into the mirror
rested. I'll leave my hair
ruffled a bit that way — fold the pyjamas,
stow the book and wash bag. Everything done,
press down the latches into the case,
that for twelve months I've watched standing out
of a morning, above the wardrobe
in a furnished room.

A Kangaroo

That hungry face
moves on grass
the way an artist's pencil
retouches
and shades.

Then, when he's bounding,
the head's borne
refined as a deer's, relaxed,
before
a powerful tight basketball attack.

And the toe-nail, in the forefront,
a stevedore's claw
(tears with it, cantilevered on his tail);
the forepaws
are a housedog's, begging.

So that here,
sitting up and simply, is the unknown
energy, which is nature,
that's able to spawn, as one,
every extreme thing.

The Farm Woman Speaks

Winter has arrived, the winds scour this place.
Feeding the children broth,
I show them now, through the dull windows,
trees rocked by a cruel cough.

We can't take a bad year,
but the lino looks like an over-ripe banana:
there's no help pacing the floors.
Leaves panic with claws on the verandah

from those trees that boom all day. Usually
you don't notice the trees' noise until night,
but if you wake then, you'd swear the sea had come
crashing inland; that awful fright

passes as you realize
where you really are, and where we are
is with crops burnt by frost, the cows
eating dry cornstalks, with all of our care

about three children and a little money
sunken here; with the pasture grass
of a morning, in this worst season for years,
thick with crushed glass —.

Of a morning, I see him let the gates fall open.
The moon thaws. Wind floats bubbles
out of a magpie — and bears upon a salver
the croak of the crows.

He jerks in boots toward the shed,
buckets pulling at his neck.
A fig tree is clenched on the earth, and strain bulges
its tendons. The fences slop either side, gone slack.

There are still the times when he will turn to me.
At night, I drowse by the persimmons in the log,
and, first, he puts an arm around me —.
Only, those flames then feel like a striding flag.

The Thief

Not the man dying for so short a time, and for such
an economic return,
and not as urgently the one there waiting
resurrection, but the other man

with these, who was simply dying — it is this one,
the pouted body
silk-white for a moment in the late afternoon,
stands above us,
while ever we feel as if there were only Jesus
splayed, in mockery of flying,
on the shaven wood.
It was not three but thousands
braced on those nails,
become rigid with agony, and lava-streaked with blood.
Speak of one other
under the leaping whips;
who was pegged there, his head wobbling like a top
     petering out;
the hair, dredged weeds;
flies in the nostrils, and strung blood in the mouth;
warped in that shape
above the city,
until there were only birds upon his bones.
We save no feeling for this pain.
On the day, people came to look,
and the guards could go through with their hammering;
they helped each other
to emblazon the thief. And for an endless time
he must have known
how sunlight slid thickly as oil amid the olive boughs,
and men reached out for wine and bread,
and dew came in the leaves
the way that stars appear. His own weight was sealing up
his lungs like
mucous lips.
People disregard this still, who never seek
in their prayers or belief
some expiation. We are only concerned
with Jesus, who is like all gods
for our gain.
Natural, no doubt, but not an end, since Jesus would
     use and condemn

a Judas, as part of His scheme. All of that
is the hollowest metaphysics we have dreamed; and all
of the thief's suffering
is ours alone.

Landscape

Thumping of the waves.
I walk, slide
subside
on the sides of
in amongst
the sandhills,
out of sight of the sea.
Here stings
like insects, on bare legs;
it's white, dry, and
lit by
a wintry sun.
The raw smell
of ocean
on such gusty day
a throat ache.
Amongst the tangle
of beach vines, juicy plump pig-face
in purple bloom;
the sand's
mottled with grey
weeds, dry and clicking,
with sulphurous
blady grass.
There are skitterings — lizards
and things
that escape with a crackle.
I turn away
and make for the railway line,
wading
dead grass, that's matted

like an old dried mop,
using a stick.
Then walking between the rails on
sleepers, shale;
the smell is soaked oil.
Either side,
as though covered with ash,
brandishing leaf and cone
weapons, the bent-kneed
banksias
in corroboree.
And I can hear now
all the silence
of the bush
dilate
on the bell-miner's
note — that lightest hammering
upon
metal, say
on this satin, polished
line. There is just
its
ding ding   *ding ding ding*

To Albert Marquet

Except for you, I'd never have known
there was such a calmness, nor where it could be found
in ordinary things: in the street's width,
on the face of a building,
on the courtyard or the field,
or on the pastures of the harbour, with the freighters
    browsing across them —
in any wide and simplifying area
seen after you.

Because to find somewhere your subject
is to feel again, on this,

how you would bring us to the border
of a shape, to its fullness,
in the precise place
where the mind has quietened, and not yet scuttled on;
is to feel some of the gentleness
with which you'd grasp it.

Much more reminds us of you,
and can involve us with what we have to see —
one finds your musical notation
among idle figures
of a promenade, or makes it from the randomness of trees
along the sky, and there's
mist in the city,
and a bridge with shadowed arches,
sunlight on the quay, or sleet upon the window,
always tugs and ferries,
they're now
as comic as small dogs, that trot in the streets
with grinning tails,
everywhere olive with yellow, mauve and grey.

Unaided, I'd have never seen
the order which one needs to find so much
lies openly here, all the time —
and yet your art puts everything in place
so easily and so freely.
One begins to look for the broadness that you looked for.
With you, we've not lost
our satisfaction in the weight of tonalities —
a harmony
that seems to be sonorous.
Although the critics hardly speak of you,
despite their systematics,
how modestly you've become
an indispensable one, to those who have such need.

Albert Marquet (1875-1947), French landscape painter: one of the
Fauves, he nevertheless maintained the tradition of Corot.

During the Bombing, 1967

Poplars, in the rainy night,
rise beyond the railway lines, scrubbed there
loosely with a brush; grey
in the purplish-greyness, that twists
above oily streets and tiles,
thorned light.
The giant hoardings and a teeming camphor laurel
crowd toward the platform's front,
a guttering spills,
as though a ruin shifted, along its length;
clatter on the concrete.
At this hour in the suburbs, I'm alone
in a draughty room;
the light is like chilled buttermilk.
'Civilian targets, formerly off-limits,
will now be bombed.' I turn it over.
'Bombing Rate "Fantastic"
Says McNamara'. Newspapers,
a magazine. This rib-separating cold —
wind forces in
and it revolves the pages for me. 'Pres. Johnson
    exhorting
support for the U.S. commitment', among other photos
of a child's running features,
a man's flesh made jelly, coming away in handfuls
with napalm, a girl's legs
blasted away. And the rain
is shattering under the awning, it blows from off
    the stone,
across the window, where my head's leaned.
I saw the last train
disappear, as I came onto the steps, but wouldn't go now
to my friends', to stand
apologetically in the porch-light,
when all they could ask was — 'China must be shown';
coffee cups on their knees, at an open fire,
and the poppies floating on the far side of the room

like out-pouring bowls.
I'll stay on
where I can keep perhaps some imagination, watching
sparks whirling
outside around the lamp-posts,
the bombs falling
on villages, as the guttering's overflowing water
falls through lightning,
here at the waiting room.

'Scattered lights ...'

Scattered lights,
one pub, and one garage.
Driving through

in the woodsmoke dusk.
A culvert
at the town limits;

the road goes on, straight,
fading. The flat
grey heath

disappearing close, on either side.
This blustery wind
brings rain — just

short hairs
of a barber's sheet,
marking the windscreen.

Morning

Feeding chickens, pollard scattered like wet sand.

They jump down stolidly from their roost
as an old sailor jumps
with wooden leg;
in there, underneath half a corrugated-iron tank,
open-ended.

I'm stepping around the bare black ground;
wire-netting propped
on lopped poles.
Moss about, bits
of brick poking through, and bones.
Rusted wrench
pressed into the ground, jaws open —
a tyrannosaurus head. Reeds.

In packing cases, one side gone, the eggs
in dry grass.
On this cold morning, they're warm, smooth:
Surprising stone

almost weightless.
Bent over;
at the side of my face, the silver
liquid paddocks, and steam.
My eyes and nose are damp, I see through my own smoke.

Finding the eggs, dry — the colour of dry sand.

Salvation Army Hostel

I'm woken up — and God knows
what's the time. It's
a woman screeching, over there
the other side of
the light-well.
I strained against the window-wire, tonight, and saw
the bottom, with rotting rag,
cardboard — a no-man's
greenish hole. And there's
evidently been rain,
surprisingly — the aftermath still
falling from a
broken gutter somewhere,
onto
that concrete
way down —
a clattering. No …
she's yelling at someone
on a floor above this who's
taking a piss, out his window —
It keeps on. He must have
got a flagon in
this place, and have his cock out through
the criss-cross
grille. A dripping
now, past me — turned over so's
to listen. I can almost see
his blind, bloated face up there
gasp.
No one else but that woman
seems awake. Who suddenly drags her window down. —
Both gone.
And I lie in the stiff, thin,
stencilled sheets
again. Like an unresolved equation;
in this aperture.

13 Poems

A waterbird lifts
out of dead grass; its slow flight
is water lapping.

Folding hessian bags
in a dim shed. From the house,
sound of crockery.

In the rock pool, grass
moves with the water. Violin bows
adagio.

Dusk. I'm scything
under trees at the front gate.
The pale moths rise.

Set a milk-bottle
out. Its tap water the same
faint shape as this moon.

The back fence, falling,
or lifted in a Hokusai wave —
the morning glory vine.

In the lane, someone
walks back with a scrap of bush,
not glancing up, at dusk.

These ripe days,
the heat, the tenderness;
a white bathtub filled with green water,
leaves against the glass.

A few cars, way off
on the freeway, over wide fields —
a lost burst of tracer fire
through the bright afternoon.

On this peak, alone;
in the wind, it feels as if my shirt
is trying to go back.

Sultry night. The moon
is small and fuzzy, an aspirin
in a glass of water.

Chopping wood,
I strike about at mosquitoes
with the axe.

Smokestack, evening sky;
and the smoke, a woman's long hair,
who pauses underwater.

Back There

A farmer in the brittle morning
struggles with solid milk cans, his gasping
all around him —

Across the yard
of scarred
mud, the tangled branches
iron lace,
and a shed is going down sideways
under convolvulus.

There's moss
on the walls
one side of the house.
A rusty plough
is stranded like the horns of a
twisted neck,
out in the mouldy
grass.

And over the raw, stripped paddocks, up
on
the windy skyline,
children run,
capering
all about that huge nerve-end,
a bare tree;
flickering, black.

On Climbing the Stone Gate Peak
(Hsieh Ling-yün, AD 385-433)

In a floating gown, I have come among these
    promontories alone;
the path is struggling on like a wounded snake.
The crags above Stone Gate are piled one upon the other:
it seems as though they will topple from out of the
    rushing mist.
All about on ledges cling the twisted pines;
all over the rocks there is moss, like a discoloured snow.
I wander into a dark copse, which the late sun pierces,
and in this gloom, a pool of scarlet water.
The haunts of ape and deer have been left behind;
only a bird now cries out mournfully, in search of its
    mate.
I climb by caves where dripping water rings like
    crystal;
and leaves of dwarf bamboo are dripping —
it is because of a waterfall thrown down, beyond here, on
    stones:
the splintering of a white jade staff.
That long pole of water goes on being shattered,
yet is no more diminished than Liu-hai with age.
Across the vibrating pool, a light smoke is windborne,
and drifts above me — the spirit of a great bird.
I climb again, breaking the cobwebs of mist;

vines are trailing from the cliffs beneath which I find my way.
Then, coming from a crevasse, gaze on other mountains.
They are blue and green inks, allowed to run upon
    slanted silk.
How could one live among such pinnacles, but with the True
    Mind,
which asks for nothing, but is open to all that is?
These rugged peaks will not prolong one gentle
    configuration,
and yet I find here strange flowers (that are struck like an
    instrument).
Only one who knows Detachment, and lets his thoughts grow
    fleeting,
could love these mountains, since his mind is not
    hampered anywhere.

The Death of Ronald Ryan

(February 3, 1967)

In the crash
pigeons on the roof
whirr
up, clattering
of wings —
visible
to the pickets beyond
those walls, who
slowly
are
at that signal
turned
around. It's done.
Grey
as Lancashire,
deserted
iron galleries.
— A revolving like a punchbag.
The dusty skylights

receive
early thin yellow
sun.
The tower clock's
nine o'clock stroke,
clang
of the trap and
his mind went flying
in the sound —
and from such tensed
sling.
To echo?
What has been done?
Some birds settling down
later
along the way back.
— Hey, there's no air here
in this bag!
You don't want
to see me —
Those pigeons
in the gravel of the
roadside
are taking hasty steps, puffed
and
eyeing us side-
ways with
eyes trembling.

Within the Traveller's Eye

A late afternoon. From this passing train
one sees the forest.
It is like a cupboard, in some deserted room,
with its door ajar.

There has been rain. Now, so late, the sunlight reappears.
We are flying low, through these small country towns. . . .

Morning glory vines grow over the wire fences
in the shape of huge snowdrifts.
Someone fat is leaning heavily on his verandah rail.

And those old pine trees in a loose main street,
where sparrows live like fleas.

We go above the mud and fallen light of an estuary;
a few birds rise.
The river, towards evening, is moving slowly
under a slow sky.

Seeing these small towns, there returns to mind
the life of a tired woman —

It is those lavatories, out in the back yards
overgrown with paspalum;
a wet cardboard box, lying about;

the piles of weathered palings stacked on trestles;
a floor-cloth, that the dog has taken.

It seems there was always this shallow afternoon light.

Steep iron roofs, old wooden places;
they face each other on gravel side streets,
with rainwater ditches out of which the grass stands,
a ramp across to each.

There is a utility moving
behind tall roadside heads of grass,

a child's white apron.

A man is walking on the long shadows
of the telegraph poles, going for cigarettes and matches
to the shop.

I know those dim, unused sitting rooms:
faint gleam of lino
among the rugs, and everything in there as rounded
as Melba's bodice.
The fringes on everything.

All through such a house was the smell of boiled
        vegetables,
and of something else
living amidst that odour —

it was the sexual hatreds, stored away
like china or cuff links,
and never spoken.
There only the daily second-best was used.

As daylight is turned low
in the grass, people by the kitchen windows,
or in the outside bathroom, at the end of a verandah,
can hear again the frogs

and crickets
begin, out in those flat, soggy paddocks.

But we have gone now miles beyond a town.
The shadow of the tallest mountain
in the valley wall

is lengthening over an empty plain of grass

we move across.

And it feels
this shadow is going to indicate, as though it were a finger,
a grave, lying open
somewhere here.

And you have to try to turn your face away.

The Pine

With a snow-cap
only
of needles;
aslant. And the lopped-off
branches of
various lengths
about its trunk.
The rhythm amongst these
such
a music, all
by chance.
Alone
in the back paddock
in the yellow grass.

Boarding House Poems

1
The landlord
standing on bare feet
saws
at the bread
in the middle of a Saturday
afternoon, to

a nasal
racing commentator's voice.
His wife
holding a cigarette
in the television room.
You go back
quietly on
the linoleum, and
the closing of
your
door.

2

Sound of traffic
outside, continuously
back and forth —
the table tennis
highway.
A sound
as if some kid
of an afternoon
is swinging viciously
right, and left,
cutting through the air
with a stick;
and a rapid bumping,
slapping noise
over the tar joins
in the concrete.
It's hot.
I lie on top of the bed
with a book.
A clock drips,
and the leaf shapes barely move
on the yellow blind.

3

Public Library
Putting a book up, moving on;
keeping hold of the one
pared volume.
Hushed,
starkly fluorescent-lit,
the air
dressed with dust.
A bald man
digs into his nose;
mustachioed man,
dog-like, in a moth-eaten overcoat; the
anxiously-peering woman.

4

Turning away
from the ladies' hairdressing salon
atmosphere
of the advertising agency —
going to work where
it's all
factories,
vacant lots, of weed and broken concrete,
terrace houses,
alleys. Down here
a light in the Italian corner shop
burns all day.
Anything feels better
for a while.
And one time
you find yourself in blunt real agreement
with someone —
that one of the other workers is officious;
'a bloody old woman'.
The taste of comradeship.

5

Lunchtimes
you see
from a bank
above the hurricane wire
a schoolboy
soccer match:
the ball
trickling smoke
all about the dry grass.
The tall chimneys
above
trailing their smoke
one way.

6

Coming in, amongst the dark wood
of the hall
early, while it's still afternoon,
you notice
the calico-looking flowers, crowded
in a vase.
How they keep on hoping.

7

Wednesday, the dead, dark
and middle of the week —
hardly redeemed
by its being pay-day;
after putting aside the rent,
straight away this evening
the most urgent job,
the washing to the laundromat.
Reading a novel,
inattentive,
on the orange polythene chair;
parched smell
of dry-cleaning fluid,
and the lifeless, dehydrated air

from spin-dryers.
During this hour, and more,
lots of times look up
and find her —
unloading bedsheets
that are like great lumps of dough
from a washing machine, or untangling
heat-blasted things,
holding the door against her side.
Intent profile
and the jeans stretched
tightly around, a
taut weight
in her shirt:
excitement
that rolls over in your stomach like
a dolphin.
And then, nothing else to do, but go,
as her air would indicate.
It's started to rain
lightly.
The rain comes undone
from a rail,
walking beside it home.
The rain is sliding
like a belt,
at an angle through the street light.
With both arms around
the large plastic bag of wash;
feeling it warm
against your body —
and the minute drops
cling
all over your face
and come stirring down, out of
your hair.

8

Rising like a clear moon,
on the wall
at the foot of my bed,
one picture — this photograph of
a Buddha;
an alert face, with a detachment like
the moon's,
with its
relentlessness.
'As Orpheus walked
amongst the forest, so you have passed
in this world:
a voice that might dispel
the beast in men.'
Lying here
I'm reminded, once again,
that it is definitely
askew.

A Labourer

He goes out early, before work, half asleep,
webs of frost on the grass; wading
paspalum to the wood-heap,
a bone-smooth axe handle pointing at him. It lifts the block
on a corner of beetled, black
earth. The logs are like rolled roasts,
they tear apart on red-fibred meat. The axe squeaks out.
Lifting it —
the head pulls backwards —
now he sinks to where he is. And the new tile roofs
encroaching about
in the thin water of the sun;
the lavatories towards here, up the back yards.
Roosters scream
through iron, spurred timber
left stand. Bringing the axe down

bounces gong-blows off the ground, raises the crows;
forging off with rusted cries
into the steam. He takes an armful of the kindling
to drop in the box beside the stove,
and splinters hang
from a red, hieroglyphed hand —
These for the child, who's father to the man;
sitting-up, so reluctantly,
in the small mist of his breakfast.

'The Single Principle of Forms'

All day a storm has fermented. Now the clouds are huge
above the mountains.

A horse stands in the paddock and swings its wooden face
at the flies.

It stands with one hind-leg poised lightly by the other,
like the way a male ballet dancer stands.

Its muzzle soggy as the stump of a freshly-cut banana
palm.

And that coarse long tail makes you think of an Indian,
waiting with a tomahawk amongst the forest.

The horse trembles its flank in the heat, and now
lightning shudders —

A silverish lightning, over those great haunches of cloud.

18 Poems

Sanding the floorboards;
across the house, in a blank window,
hibiscus flowers.

The umbrella,
a crushed insect; in the sleet
on a drifting canal.

On the enamel dish, slice open
a pear.
Rain hangs in the window gauze.

Late afternoon.
Clouds that might be Kilimanjaro
from the dry savanna.

Soaking in the hot bath;
on a radio somewhere
the time-pips. Three o'clock.

I get up. It's bright
moonlight. The sea, a glass brimming
underneath the tap.

Some children's voices,
a piano, in the hollow School of Arts.
In the alley, rain floats.

Long wet verandah,
leaves blown in. Our souls could live
nowhere but the Earth.

Hot night. In the yard,
tighten the tap. It still drips.
The mosquitoes come.

Stone jug filled
with milk, and two bubbles
like an igloo.

Passing on a train;
sheets borne out from a clothes-line
and the pasture-land.

Huge, glittering stars.
Looking up, out among the frogs'
croaking, croaking.

The new moon —
fallen out of its gown,
a white breast.

The rain, soft and everywhere,
becomes cricket calls
crackling, popping, in the loam.

Walking in high forest;
a swallow   blown away
from a crest of the trail.

In the city
the unexceptional night —
small change.

A drop hung
indoors, from the tap's blunt
beak. A bird sings.

Burnt-out cornstalks askew
in the wet.
Standing hooded with a sack
amongst a battle's aftermath
long ago.

The Meatworks

Most of them worked around the slaughtering
out the back, where concrete gutters
crawled off
heavily, and the hot, fertilizer-thick,
sticky stench of blood
sent flies mad,

but I settled for one of the lowest-paid jobs, making mince
right the furthest end from those bellowing,
sloppy yards. Outside, the pigs' fear
made them mount one another
at the last minute. I stood all day
by a shaking metal box
that had a chute in, and a spout,
snatching steaks from a bin they kept refilling
pushing them through
arm-thick corkscrews, grinding around inside it,
    meat or not —
chomping, bloody mouth —
using a greasy stick
shaped into a penis.
When I grabbed it the first time
it slipped, slippery as soap, out of my hand,
in the machine
that gnawed it hysterically a few moments
louder and louder, then, shuddering, stopped;
fused every light in the shop.
Too soon to sack me —
it was the first thing I'd done.
For a while, I had to lug gutted pigs
white as swedes
and with straight stick tails
to the ice rooms, hang them by the hooves
on hooks — their dripping
solidified like candle-wax — or pack a long intestine
with sausage meat.
We got meat to take home —
bags of blood;
red plastic with the fat showing through.
We'd wash, then
out on the blue metal
towards town; but after sticking your hands all day
in snail-sheened flesh,
you found, around the nails, there was still blood.
I usually didn't take the meat.

I'd walk home on
the shiny, white-bruising beach, in mauve light,
past the town.
The beach, and those startling, storm-cloud mountains, high
beyond the furthest fibro houses, I'd come
to be with. (The only work
was at this Works.) — My wife
carried her sandals, in the sand and beach grass,
to meet me. I'd scoop up shell-grit
and scrub my hands,
treading about
through the icy ledges of the surf
as she came along. We said that working with meat was like
burning-off the live bush
and fertilizing with rottenness,
for this frail green money.
There was a flaw to the analogy
you felt, but one
I didn't look at, then —
the way those pigs stuck there, clinging onto each other.

To The Master, Dōgen Zenji
(1200-1253 AD)

Dōgen came in and sat on the wood platform;
all the people were gathered
like birds upon the lake.

After years, home from China,
and he had brought no scriptures; he showed them
empty hands.

This in Kyoto,
at someone-else's temple. He said, All that's important
is the ordinary things.

Making a fire
to boil the bathwater, pounding rice, pulling weeds
and knocking dirt from their roots,

or pouring tea — those blown scarves,
a moment, more beautiful than the drapery
in paintings by a master.

'It is this world
of the *dharmas* (the momentary particles)
that is the Diamond.'

•

Dōgen received, they say, his first insight
from the old cook of some monastery
in China,

who was on the jetty
where they docked, who had come down
to buy mushrooms

among the rolled-up
straw sails, the fishnets, brocade litters,
and geese in baskets.

High sea-going junk,
shuffling and dipping
like an official.

Dōgen could see
an empty shoreline, the pinewood plank of the beach,
the mountains

far off
and dusty. Standing about
with his new smooth skull.

The horses' lumpy hooves clumped on those planks,
they arched their necks
and dipped their heads like swans,

manes blown about
like white threads from off
the falling breakers;

holding up their hooves as though they were tender,
the sea grabbing at
the timber below.

And the two Buddhists in all the shuffle got to bow.
The old man told him, Up there,
that place —

The monastery a cliff-face
in one of the shadowy hills.
My study is cooking;

no, not devotion. No,
no, not your sacred books (meaning Buddhism). And Dōgen,
irate —

he must have thought
who is this old prick, so ignorant
of the Law,

and it must have shown.
Son, I regret
that you haven't caught on

to where it is one discovers
the Original Nature
of the mind and things.

•

Dōgen said, Ideas
from reading, from people, from a personal bias,
toss them all out —

'discolourations'.
You shall only discover by looking in
this momentary mind.

And said, 'The Soto school
isn't one
of the entities in Buddhism —

don't even use such names.'
The world's an incessant transformation, and to meditate
is awareness, with no

clinging to,
no working on, the mind.
It is a floating; ever-moving; 'marvellous emptiness'.

Only absorption in such a practice will release us
from the accidents, and appetites,
of life.

And upon this leaf one shall cross over
the stormy sea,
among the dragon-like waves.

Bright Day

The fantail is tying
loosely
a complex knot,
as if as an illustration,
about one spot
in the air

and then drawing it sharp;
yanked-tight
noose
on some frailer string —
the tangled line
in the sun
of a beetle, or other living thing;

throttling it.
It chops that end
short, and
this fantail, in its mantilla —
the swirling,
the blur —
goes off once more, taut;
not far

Again,
like some applause-igniting
artistry,
it flourishes a
variation
on that elaborate bow —
is adding, everywhere,
its satin
finishing touches to the morning.

15 Poems

You forgot the flowers,
I have kept them in a jar.
It smells as if you're here.

I'm getting up later —
these stormy nights of autumn.
Sailboats on the lake.

4 a.m.; the Milky Way
blown along, high over the forest.
A truck changes down.

Rainy weather
with the light on all day.
Like waiting for someone.

Daytime movie;
and coming outside, it's dark.
I turn another way.

So hot, the sparrow looks ill —
sitting on the tap handle.

Lean in the wash-up,
trying a poem. On the dark
window, scratches of rain.

Sunday morning,
wandering to the bathroom;
it's filled with sunlight.

Weary, I tear open the shopping.
From newspaper waddles
on the table
like an irate duck
this melon.

The pleasure of weeds:
to see them beneath the street-lights.

I thought it was rain,
and sat up in the dark to listen —
Only falling leaves.

The train's halted
nowhere. Small birds whirling up
from the dry grass.

Drunk last night; waking
with limbs scattered on the bed. . . .
The shiny leaves move.

Sunken grave, iron,
come upon, trampling long grass.
Rain-drop sliding down.

A melon, overlooked
out in the muddy paddocks —
it's all right.

The Sawmill Shacks

The shacks are overgrown on the mountainside
we come rattling around
in Ted's bomb. A dirt road,
metal clang
under the car; the trail
to a waterfall.
Silent, chill
bush below,
the tree-tops tattered,
smoke-blue; high,
shot-to-pieces shapes against a frail
wintry sky. Halfway
on the cold

volcano, as steep
as sawdust
under a chute, once, in this dead
(oil-dirt and rusty cog)
crawled-through town.
At the top of the dry creek-bed of the street,
a furnace: rusted
cone with a round
tip, its sieve-like
smoke vent. An old Chev
timber truck's sunk
like a bullock down, almost gone,
blind.
The stores and shacks
are shingled weatherboard,
lines scored,
their boards curling
away. Huge ferns
spout through the boardwalks and
fungus is spreading everywhere, like bright
dried apricot.

Just out, above the road,
the Community Hall,
weathered salmon-pink, slipping
through weeds, some planks held by
one nail.
Inside,
a boarded-up gloom, dust
in the door-beam
on the breathless floor,
furry.
A hollowness,
splattered with bird-lime. There's
a book on the floor, flaked
to rusty shale —
Baroness Orczy,
'property of
the C.W.A.' And a Sunday school print
on the wall: a saint bestowing

rhetorical blessing,
smouldering, through the nicotine-coloured
stain.
A piano, with the seeming grin
of old bones:
caries, and the teeth's
enamel gone. . . .

You hear the rudimentary violin;
stamping boots
and a sudden dog-like yelp; tea cups scrape;
the whining, dogmatic women's voices,
and their squawks;
a bellowing, out of florid jowls; those songs
of places they could hardly imagine:
Sacramento,
no doubt, and San Antonio,
and one would have been Phoenix. . . .

Gladys, Clarrie, Madge and Arthur:
concerned about
the hint
of a slight —
with our mind, that is too often like
a knocked-over
hive.
So little to do, anywhere here,
but resume;
their lives become a long time.
Women who'd cry
without finding any tears,
who startled themselves, wondering where this was;
those men
who did not pause at twilight,
whose solution was to put on
a snarl;
people the same as any —
blown away
out of a stony, slanted gap.

They have got lost again, somewhere.
On the mouth
a taste of pity, thinking of us.
The rafters are clotted with nests
and, treading about,
from inside the piano
a dead-animal stench. You have to push out,
under cobwebs
(the door-screech), stepping
jerkily in thin sun. And a crow lurches away
slides down
far off
we soar
over the vague blue mountainside. . . .
How the tree-tops there
like wave crests
glint
in the last, reaching,
spatulate beams. And this huge dome

of air:
navy-blue, porous; the
blue of endless-
ness.
Inside your chest, you feel yourself arising. —
Other mountains
far along from here, like skyscrapers
at dusk
with all of their lights out,
in the faint mist.
This opened-up
melon, of the evening.

Out here,
the long grasses
are swirled
loosely
like a buoy.
And now the stars,

the first few,
clear
as water
on a grass blade,
appearing,
effortless
as stars appear. . . .

But we catch ourselves standing about. — It is
a sound of water
underneath the groaning of this
tethered avalanche —
the piled-up
heights of the forest —
everywhere.
And all that trickling water
seems an evil sound, in such a place:
speaks of
black, icy leaf-mulch
that it sinks through; and of spreading over bald,
    slimy ground;
of the roots
standing out, furry, from frozen soil
like rib-cages;
a
deranged scrawl
of sharp-toothed lantana
where only it can pass —
in the enormous day-long gloom
behind those torrential lines
of forest.

As if for a ballet,
all the light has fallen out of the sky,
and cold rears up,
the wind rises from the left.
Hard to see
the timber-getters' shacks,
each as lightless and empty,

as cast-off,
as a skull; staved-in.
This cold!
It reveals to you, like a disease, the shape of your bones.
Stumble down,
and now the headlights are swung solidly about
on the dank
cellar of leeches. —
Feeling our way
through all four wheels of the car
out
into the long valley. And
dropping here

easily as an owl glides,
across these paddocks upholstered in
    powdery weeds. —
The moon's
now fully risen,
afloat
in an immense fine spray
like perfume,
filling all the valley.
And one already said of nature
it is not 'human-hearted'; except that, in men it is,
in some men.
Whatever is added to nature
nature's made.
Dimly you feel
out of what endless dissatisfactions
we have come.

North Coast Town

Out beside the highway, first thing in the morning,
nothing much in my pockets but sand
from the beach. A Shell station (with their Men's locked),
a closed hamburger stand.

I washed at a tap down beside the changing sheds,
stepping about on mud. Through the wall
smell of the vandals' lavatory,
and an automatic chill flushing in the urinal.

Eat a floury apple, and stand about. At this kerb
sand crawls by, and palm fronds here
scrape dryly. Car after car now — it's like a boxer
warming-up with the heavy bag, spitting air.

A car slows and I chase it. Two hoods
going shooting. Tattoos and greasy fifties pompadour.
Rev in High Street, drop their first can.
Plastic pennants on the distilled morning, everywhere;

a dog trotting, and someone hoses down a pavement;
our image flaps in shop fronts; smoking on
past the pink 'Tropicana' motel (stucco, with sea shells);
the RSL, like a fancy-dress Inca; the 'Coronation',

a warehouse picture show. We pass
bulldozed acres. The place is becoming chrome,
tile-facing, and plate-glass: they're making California.
Pass an Abo, not attempting to hitch, outside town.

Grass Script

Late Ferry

The late ferry is leaving now;
I stay to watch
from the balcony, as it goes up onto
the huge dark harbour,

out beyond that narrow wood jetty;
the palm tree tops
make a sound like touches
of the brush on a snare drum

in the windy night. Going beyond
street lights' fluorescence
over the dark water, a ceaseless
activity, like chromosomes

uniting and dividing. And out beyond
the tomato stake patch
of the yachts, with their orange
lights; leaving this tuberous

small bay, for the city
across an empty dark. There, neon
redness trembles down in the water
as if into ice, and

the longer white lights
feel nervously about in the blackness,
towards here, like hands
after the light switch.

The ferry wades now into the broad
open harbour, to be lost soon
amongst a silver blizzard of light
swarming below the Bridge:

a Busby Berkeley spectacular
with thousands in frenzied, far-off

choreography, in their silver lamé,
the Bridge like a giant prop.

One does seem in a movie theatre:
that boat is small as a moth
wandering through the projector's beam,
seeing it float beneath the city.

I'll lose sight of the ferry soon —
I find it while it's on darkness
and savour it like honeycomb,
filled as it is with its yellow light.

The Name

He is a man getting on
in years,

who listens to racing
at the pub

when he finishes work
about 2.00.

Or he'll come straight back
sometimes

to the room. I can hear
he's lying down

again,
to use the name

of a woman
who has forgotten him.

Old House

In the long, windy grass
on the headland,
against a deep sea,
the closed wooden house, with its verandahs
and observatory.

The roller blinds are drawn;
a late sun throws
the shadow
of railing and bars, onto the weatherboards,
askew.

All that grass is rippling, the way hounds
undulate
on the scent. Out to sea
only the cold hoofprints of the light
are left. A white yacht.

The yacht appeared from amongst
the wrung grass
of the slope,
silently,
and is folded back now, along the coast.

The crack of its going-about,
and the cry
of a gull, echoed
in the bare verandah.
Down an institution's corridor, a white coat.

Poem to Kristina

1

Remembering a time, on sandy wheel tracks,
amongst all that sharp hot machinery, the bush. —
Your flouncing, tired walk;
coming back, feet puffing up the dust,
carrying your sandals;
petulant, grizzling, and laughing with me about it,
but still close to anger,
and knowing that I knew.
I can see myself trying to be humorous for you.

2

Amongst the rocks, I broke open
and persuaded you about your first oyster,
also. Talking like a cage full of birds, and
posing, gesturing, like a samurai,
to get your courage, you swallowed it
and with a scream leapt up
onto the sudden bracket of my arms,
and clung there wriggling your legs, and squealing,
and laughing out something. You liked it.

3

Your face, so often, ready to take offence;
defensive, hurt, if my eyes flickered
away while you talked all your unsure rush of talk.
Or else, you presented it with those hours of
barely any make-up. Posed, as playful and artificial
as photos of Marilyn. Which made me feel
your human 'mirror
mirror on the wall' — a responsive mirror
of flesh, for you to confirm, with my startled look,
what you'd found in the glass one.

4

At night, you wouldn't use the outdoor lavatory
last thing, for fear of spiders. And for fear

of the dark, you made me come outside
so you could pee. You bared your cream cheese
behind, beneath the clothes-line, and would remark
about all the tree of stars,
with your brown thighs splayed apart, like Havana cigars.

5

On grey days, out the kitchen window,
we watched the grey water moving by in the lake —
a crowd through turnstiles. Mooching about,
listening to our few records over and over;
in the half-light of the house, their combed Valentino sheen.
Making sandwiches at the sink, and putting on,
after enquiry, the Tim Buckley, or an Otis Redding, or
     Van Morrison.
And sitting there, leaned together,
like two horses out in the yard in the rain.

6

Now I sit and look back. And we write sometimes;
we keep in touch, as they say.
I remember those times when I was happy
and didn't think I was. Strange, the way
only now I recognize it
as happiness. That that should be what happiness is like.
Too late, as people say.
It's true. — The worst is, you begin to suspect
there's to be realized, in life,
a homily as often
as we did not believe.

In the Bus

    In the back of an old country bus, down a bitumen side
road through the floating rain. All the school kids dropped
off, we're going on to the next town; and now you can hear the
frying-pan splutter underneath and the flap of wipers.
    On a rattling wood bridge we slow to look at the yellow
creek rising; water coming over some usually dry large stones,

where there's foam like a curtain-end beating out of a window. And through a paper mill forest — here every pine, I realize, will have this shredded lank grey water all over it, delicately as pollen upon a stamen.

Going on, to the shouted speculations of a couple of women, a farm worker and the driver; the puddles in the aisle throwing a straight punch on the corners; the steamy smell of wet wool. The rubbed-off windows are again grey, and on their outside is pebbled water, that trembles like the face of a honeycomb covered with bees.

Although, there is the teeming green of the bush wherever a trickle of water has seeped in, and is moving down the glass like some small water-tufted animal that goes slowly along out there oblivious, keeping its head down all about the ground in the rain.

The Chair

Sitting out
a chair in the garden
morning sun
fine gravel among
outbreaks of flowering bush
ferns
a twisted surging white
log
lain in the open
the waterlily
stepping stones

Roof crackling in the heat
bird claws
all over it
this one-time farmhouse
a stain
like a grazed shinbone

on its long slide
tin

I see the grey-brown
fine bowled-over grass
in flat paddocks
fences
stitching it all
corroded smoky line of the bush
one coil
of the scaly river

And have to go back in
too hot
the chair's left standing
out
in the blazing yard
wooden
looming
in the sun

I can see it through these glass doors
in moving about
the hot shadowy house
getting up to spray flies
or to get a drink
the chair is standing its ground

And I want to sleep
I would like to be a seed
deep in the earth
I want
a dream of water
lying
in the mouth
a creek that rises
into a cave under the bank
and to wake at nightfall

when the autumn is already coming on
leaves falling

The chair will be standing outside still
the fallen leaves
upon it
it is like a working-man
bringing for me the basket
in his arms

Greyhounds

Bobbing of balloons
held by a string. On the tips of claws
click,
clickclick
softly. The pack
blown awry
easily, like a spread newspaper in
the elbowing wind.

Surely they are meant for some deviousness,
not that
full-pelt anxiety to kill.

Thus, they are such subtle animals:
an emblem
for the successful man.

— In the race
all obsequiousness or restraint gone;
they jack-knife up and down,
jockeying
upon a blast or slipstream
that's lifting them off their feet.

Whirling around under the lamp's roar.

They get their teeth out.

You meet them in the street at night;
a soft flickering
again.
In the hands of preoccupied men
who fling aside the cigarette butts,
hurry and scheme;
who don't show them any love.

These dogs adapt
to anything, in the pursuit
of their own nature.

They lope right over the proffered
turds of other dogs.

I see them coming,
being given to walking about late;
and hear my footsteps
failing, as I approach, in this long street,
the lit, empty
telephone box.

'The old wooden venetian blinds ...'

The old wooden venetian blinds are closed. I put my
case down and open them with an arm I can hardly raise.
The backyard's a scrawl of paspalum, just large enough for
a rusted rotary clothes hoist.

The shafts of light coming into the room are like
the city's escalators in rows, with this dust drifting along
them. . . .

Poem to my Father

Dear father, you were buried
   in perfect summer weather.
      Such a day
you would sit outdoors
   and put your bad leg up
      in its slipper,
and pretend not to like it there:
   too crowded
      on the porch, with the pot plants,
or too shady,
   or too hot;
      you would call out
to my mother and sister
   and make them run;
      you'd have your lunch brought
on a tray, with doilies
   and frangipani,
      presented
for you to fault.

Though, some found that day too hot,
   and you could sympathize:
      old-timers
from the RSL;
   those red-faced
      mates of yours, dabbing
with handkerchiefs
   at hat-band welts,
      the purple onion-root
in nostrils,
   cheeks,
      flaring urgently as
heat lightning at night.

I told myself, your father
   is in the rank grass,
      who gave you body and soul.

That is why I've searched
    anxiously
        your face
propped on the hospital pillows —
    for some trait
        like the corridor
of a dank hotel
    at the end of which is
        hung
a verandah, in the open.

I've found
    such fine bones
        in your face —
you have them yet.
    What one might only wish to keep
        of you, you keep,
also.
    In you, now signifying nothing;
        although
that chemistry was ineffectual,
    always —
        overcome
by some other gene
    or something infancy had done.
        That's all there is to say.

That's all.
    But everything you did once
        we thought against us.
The money you borrowed,
    won with
        and lost again.
All those days you went to get blind,
    so well turned out.
        The condemnation
in a haughty voice
    at every meal

of my books, my hopeless maths,
my choice of sport.
    (I was the eldest
        and had to sit beside you.)
It didn't matter to you there was no
    Rugby Union,
        I ought to be playing it;
I was letting you down.

Who was this
    thin-faced, hollow,
        neurasthenic devil,
with his ulcers,
    at the table with us?
        To whom everything was distasteful.
Mocking.
    How bad-tempered you looked
        after your close
fortnightly haircut.
    I could outrun you, and I needed to,
by the time I was eleven.

And we ran out
    at night
        when it was past the time
you should be home —
    at our mother's intuition
        prodding
under the lantana
    along the road.
        We'd find you
with the bottles emptied
    that you, already drunk, had decided
        you were going to bring.
Once you began
    you'd keep on
        until the blessed, regular
Repat. Hospital interments.

But the day after
　　you would get up,
shave painfully, polish your shoes to righteousness,
　　and walk in the house
　　　　'looking for trouble';
an excuse for another
　　departure,
　　　　to spend the precious
TPI pension —
The Money.

I remember
　　our pathetic pride
　　　　to see you dressed again
and walking in the main street
　　of that town
　　　　as if you owned the place —
'Such a hide,'
　　my mother said; she would look angry,
　　　　and almost smile.
We were those sun-browned,
　　skinny,
　　　　bare-foot, bike-riding
small animals
　　whom you ignored.
　　　　It didn't worry us, for long;
we ran wild;
　　we were all right
　　　　so long as you weren't around.

Some might have thought
　　you wanted to play the rake,
　　　　yet it was always
without panache —
　　with no verve, no enjoyment,
　　　　no gaiety,
that we could ever see.
　　With a determined, thin-lipped
　　　　selfishness.

What went wrong
    when you were young? It was nothing
     exceptional
        that I can find.
So, you will become now
    in your children's lives,
        sometimes,
just the half-conscious, troubling
    sense of something
        we have forgotten to do,
or to bring
    along with us,
        if anything wants to remind us
of you.
    You have gone
        as if you were an illusion.

Although, my mother weeps.
    It is real;
        she loved you
when she could.
    Your second wife, she got religion
        and stayed.
What was going to happen
    to you
        otherwise?
She took in washing,
    worked as a cleaner,
        and got all of us by.
The closest I saw you together,
    the most affectionate,
        she was holding your hand
cutting the fingernails.
    You were embarrassed,
        hurrying her.
She wanted to play.
She was then past fifty.

Dear father,
   you did everything badly;
      the most
'difficult patient'
   in the nursing home.
      Poor man.
I cannot believe
   your wretchedness
      on all the occasions I recall.
If I think of you
   I'm horrified — I become obsessed
      with you. It is like
love.
   I am filled with pity.
      I want to live.

Pumpkins

What in novels is called 'a grizzled stubble'
on these pumpkin leaves.
The leaves shuffle
as you wade amongst them, their bristles
rustling.
One is slowly stepping upon
egg shells,
pagodas of orange peel,
on heaps of tea slops.
And the pumpkin flower,
a big loud daffodil.
You push about darkness, parting the leaves.
A rooster is on this slope, also;
come to peck
outside, in the late afternoon.
It is putting down its spur
with care,
and its eye is flickering about.
The rooster is red
and lacquered as a Chinese box;

a golden hood
down to its shoulders, like a calyx, flexible
upon its body, as it pecks,
flicks,
flicks, and blinks,
pecks. I'm holding one foot up, looking for
somewhere
amongst this vine. And find
the pumpkin —
segmented like a peeled mandarin
or leather
on the back seat of a thirties tourer.
I break the stem
and lift the heavy, warped pumpkin,
just when the vine's become
too dark.
In between pink and yellow,
its orange tone
can be added easily to the sunset
that's been going on.
I take the pumpkin beneath my arm.
Like a bad painting, this magnificent sunset.

Looking After a Friend's House

I wake sometime towards daybreak,
hold apart
the curtains, propping myself up,
and can see the moon
setting.

It's down behind the stand
of distant bare trees — those torn bits
of flyscreen
tacked
onto sticks.

The moon is settling
quickly, the way an egg yolk
slides along
and off
a table top.

It shines across
these paddocks, with their dark
turned-over clods.
In some of the hollows, in the moonlight,
water lies.

I reach back and
press the light switch, to keep on
reading. And read
until there glides up against me what seems
an icy cat.

Drab as goat's milk,
the first daylight. I hunch down, and feel myself
dissolving.
And next, sunlight is heavy on the quilt,
I am under all the dust-motes.

Now this light will be inside, shoved right through

the house, cycling down
onto linoleum.
And I hear the refrigerator starting up again
in the bare kitchen.

'Smoke of logs ...'

Smoke of logs and drifting rain out in the paddocks.
The rolling paddocks are long grey waves, far at sea,
beneath this blowing rain. And the dark line of bush, a
crowd of emigrants at the rail.

Afterwards

A photo of you
against the turmoil

towards the end of
the wedding day,

holding for your
young brother's snap-shot

his pocket money's
gift,

a
kitchen knife.

You smile,
so open-

faced, into his camera,
shining and

holding out
the gaudy

Woolworths
cello-fronted box.

Flushed and posing,
innocent.

This picture
that still can make me

catch my breath and
turn away,

as if I saw my flesh
part

underneath a drawn
knife-blade.

Tropical Morning

I roll over and wake. The light
is like a divorce photograph. And a sharp
bird-note
pierces beneath the verandah's deep

frontal lobe. Sit up to face
the sky, an infinite
cruel calm. Trees in this place
feathered bones. And the cliff, a brute

relic, re-emerging over
tin roofs. This light, with its copious dust
swirling, burrows for cover indoors.
The underside of a crust,

one's sheet. Another alarmed call. That alert
sentry, a weapon in its face, was here:
it came in the verandah's slit,
and has leapt again on the swollen air.

The Visit

Blown onto the coast road, I go to see my mother,
unexpectedly.

I walk down the same dirt country street
with duffle bag,

and find her in the garden; her prolapsed belly.
She is grey — so grey.

Her hands, lined with the garden dirt,
fly to her face, and hair.

Straight away, she must think of something to eat.
On back steps, wintry sunlight gossip.

I play some old records. Where I left has grown over.
My brother comes for lunch

and on the quiet he tells me she is not so good.
She does become tired suddenly,

'because of the shock', and has to rest.
I wake her last thing,

late in the afternoon. I must be in Brisbane tomorrow;
must catch the bus. Her soft loose skin.

But I'll write. She says that she won't worry
now she's seen me. Reaching up.

I go out, to grab a book I remember I have left here,
find her sleeping again.

Flames and Dangling Wire

On a highway over the marshland.
Off to one side, the smoke of different fires in a row,
like fingers spread and dragged to smudge:
it is an always-burning dump.

Behind us, the city
driven like stakes into the earth.
A waterbird lifts above this swamp
as a turtle moves on the Galapagos shore.

We turn off down a gravel road,
approaching the dump. All the air wobbles
in some cheap mirror.
There is a fog over the hot sun.

Now the distant buildings are stencilled in the smoke.
And we come to a landscape of tin cans,
of cars like skulls,
that is rolling in its sand dune shapes.

Amongst these vast grey plastic sheets of heat,
shadowy figures
who seem engaged in identifying the dead —
they are the attendants, in overalls and goggles,

forking over rubbish on the dampened fires.
A sour smoke
is hauled out everywhere,
thin, like rope. And there are others moving — scavengers.

As in hell the devils
might pick about through our souls, for vestiges
of appetite
with which to stimulate themselves,

so these figures
seem to wander, disconsolate, with an eternity

in which to turn up
some peculiar sensation.

We get out and move about also.
The smell is huge,
blasting the mouth dry:
the tons of rotten newspaper, and great cuds of cloth. . . .

And standing where I see the mirage of the city
I realize I am in the future.
This is how it shall be after men have gone.
It will be made of things that worked.

A labourer hoists an unidentifiable mulch
on his fork, throws it in the flame:
something flaps
like the rag held up in 'The Raft of the Medusa'.

We approach another, through the smoke,
and for a moment he seems that demon with the long
    barge pole.
— It is a man, wiping his eyes.
Someone who worked here would have to weep,

and so we speak. The rims beneath his eyes are wet
as an oyster, and red.
Knowing all that he does about us,
how can he avoid a hatred of men?

Going on, I notice an old radio, that spills
its dangling wire —
and I realize that somewhere the voices it received
are still travelling,

skidding away, riddled, around the arc of the universe;
and with them, the horse-laughs, and the Chopin
which was the sound of the curtains lifting,
one time, to a coast of light.

The Calm

Early morning:
it grows light in the bedroom
but is still shadowy

because of the clouds
like quilting.
It is a cool, firm-fleshed

young morning,
the bird-song random and brief
as wind chimes.

The light makes strange corridors
in this polished, plain
wardrobe.

The sound of a train along
the mountain
quite clear, beyond the quiet town;

a train going through deep blue cuttings
in the rock
and among the blue trees.

The curtains here
long gowns, under which the feet of
the breeze

prance
their few steps and
slide back.

One could have the bedlight on
to read, but would miss
this smoke-

soft
change of light.
The leaves are stirring like something

in a calm sea.
I get up, pulling my pyjamas together,
see where the newspaper

has slid across the lawn.
A dark blue hose is coiled,
bright dandelions

beside it, drawn
around in the seed-tops
of the grass. All this, so vivid

on a grey spring morning.
I lie down
again, under the one frail

sheet; lie still,
not thinking. Listening to the quietness.
And I hear someone else is up,

moving about,
that now in the bathroom the tap
is running, like a wound.

The Swallows

A 100-yard square reservoir is sunk in the open field
amongst the long, wind-drawn grass.
Rusty hurricane wire
surrounds this wide place, and beyond it one sees
some blocks of flats
that are like punched cards.
All the grass that we are wading into is sat upon by the wind
at once, and then it straightens

as if to breathe
and goes down again, in a slightly different direction.
There are smoke stacks against a charcoal view,
and five great cooling towers, overlapping,
with pipe-smoke seeping across the lips of some.
A very tall antenna — a pure line —
is ruled up into another part of the sky:
a knife-blade, portioning
the vat of bluish, watery skim cheese.
And here, everywhere above the pale brown reservoir's
chipped water,
the swallows are flickering;
a large flock, that is like scratchings upon an old film
of the Midlands town below.
Going closer, the swallows seem black scraps of paper that
    whirl and turn
over a bonfire.
Their rubbery wings
are like long, narrow fins, and they plane down on these
fast, twittering them alternately.
We flinch and duck — amused,
startled, at the way they have begun dive-bombing us.
Little pronged, sharp tails,
and porpoise-shaped bodies, splay-beaked.
They are bouncing and rebounding all about the air.
These juddering bats,
diving at us, continuously, and planing off.
And beyond them now, a Choral Vision —
the cathedral window strainings, through smoky air,
of late afternoon sun.
The sun is gathered into a bouquet of stage lights
on the English countryside, that is like a golf course,
on gas tanks, and on the cold tea
of the cramped river.
And these darkening swallow shapes
have been reduced, each, to a symbol —
they are just a quarter moon with an arrow crossing;
that symbol on many dozen

churned-about flags — stretched,
or snapping, or falling in the wind.
There is such an eloquent, fervent demonstration on
    this hilltop.
It's something ritualized and ancient
with exuberant life —
something, outside the museums, that can overcome
the sharp play
of the visitors' deflation.

10 Poems

White rowboat,
slowest wingbeat. A hotel window's
flower-patterned air.

Cold afternoon fields;
the lights of a roadside shop
fill the puddles.

Figures racing to the surf
strike the silver water, crooked
as roots of ginger.

Mountainside dusk,
white flowers scattered in the bush —
the milking-shed lights.

The station master,
gazing across the wide, hot flats,
pours tea-leaves on the tracks.

Verandah rail
and above, a stripe of ocean.
The clouds' stage.

Drying her eyes,
outside on the hilltop street;
hiding in the wind.

At the cafeteria
a few people, and all the table-tops
in wide morning light.

In a window, early,
the city, across the harbour,
or stumps of a gully
in the smoky morning bush.

The torch beam
I feel with, through the pouring night,
is smoke.

Dharma Vehicle

1

Out of the reach of voices
in the wind.

Camping at a fibro shack
fishermen use —
swept with tea-tree branches, and washed down
with kerosene tins of
tank water.

Like banners raised,
all these eucalyptus saplings —
the straight trees.

A sea-breeze
over the grass headland, where fallen, white
branches swim;
leaves here
are shaken all the time,
shoes that run
on stone.

My bed
a pile of cut fern.

•

And the Pacific Ocean mornings
in windows rinsed with
wet handkerchief,
among the whitish-grey, ragged paperbarks —

that glint
all over,
in long shoals,

of translucent
scales.

At night,
lying by the fire
outdoors — seeming to lean above
moon and stars afloat.

The distant cannon
of the waves. . . .

The paperbarks climb
slowly,
and are spreading out, like incense-smoke.

•

I read beneath the trees all day,
caught-up
with those old Chinese
who sought the right way to live, and found
one must adapt to nature,
to what is
outside our egotism;
who loved this earth.

'Here I am
gulping the stuff from the fountain
and willing to let it
trickle out of my mouth.'   (Lucretius)

In India, the Buddhists
praised insensibility
to the world
('Doth not the Hindoo
lust after vacuity?');
but with Buddhism's arrival in China,
by the T'ang,
in the time of Hui-neng, the sixth
patriarch, there'd come

a complete reversal of such *dharma* —

There is the Other Shore,
it is here.

•

It is not reaching into any deep centre,
but to awaken the mind without fixing it
    anywhere.

A man who goes into trance
and has no thought or feeling   (Hui-neng)
surely is no better than a block of stone
or bit of wood.

But to know pleasure as pleasure
and pain as pain
and to keep the mind free from all attachment
is what's called No-Thought.

•

I turn out the lamp.
Leaves, twigs, berries falling
on the tin like rain
in the night.
— It was the monk
Fa Ch'an-ang, in China,
dying,
heard a squirrel screech
out on the moon-wet tiles, and who told them
'It's only this.'

•

Only this.
A wide flat banana leaf,
wet green,
unbroken, leaning on
the glass.

The mother-of-pearl of a cloudy dawn.

2

How shall one continue
to confront every morning
this same face in the mirror?

Anxiously peering,
demanding —
such intolerable self-pity;

hysterical, and without decency.
Impossible marriage
with such a face, that eats up other people.

I do not want to be this sort of cripple
in the world any longer;
not for any of my excuses for being

to remain,
not for any of my possibilities.
I do not want to be what I am.

I'm woken here,
I would like simply to walk away.
And live without saying that I live,

without me
as the filament, the grains, the sedimentary content,
the matter to be taken into account.

And continue,
but without this continuing; certainly,
not to remain defender of such a proposition,

which, every next moment, life is going to contradict,
and with the back of its hand,
and with its fist.

•

When you are suffering
and you want to be free
of that which torments you,

it is not greed,
is it?
This is something more basic than

the calculations of thought.
And this is why I've felt
it's possible

to elude the mind,
whose confusion has continued
for too long.

The summer's almost gone.

3

The holymen whom Gautama sought-out in the forest —
torment of a leper —
knew about Transience,
as did Heraclitus, about this time,
but taught there is a soul,
Atman,
'I',
and that it's the same as the World-Soul, Brahman,
of abiding nature.
Gautama saw there is no cure for the Self
in such belief.

'I saw the thorn
that is piercing to the heart of men' —
and belief in the soul is part of its poison —
the thorn
is one's subjective desire,
to which a man clings above all,
tenacious like the shark
and as cruel —

'If this thorn is drawn out
one is calm and knows peace.'

He could not find his relief among those *sannyasin*,
and so, went on alone;
staring in
where all the other's knees had failed them —
on the edge of the buffalo pasture
in blue smoke of moonlight,
in the wet grass,
with mud running on his body;
or among tree roots,
and there he saw the ragged wild flight
of the stars,
a particular night —
it was like,
as many others have said, since then,
'the bottom falling out
of the washtub',
or
'like flowers suddenly blooming
on withered trees'.

•

'No God, so soul' —
It is all like a mountain river,
travelling very far, and very swiftly;
not for a moment does it cease to flow.
One thing disappears and determines what is arising,
and there is no unchanging substance
through all of this,
nothing to call permanent,
only Change.
That which is the substance of things
abides as nothing
and has nowhere
a nature of its own.
Its essential nature is Nothingness.

•

In Western thought, this recalls something that Engels said
in 'Dialectics of Nature' —
that 'motion is the mode of existence
of matter';
there is no form of matter that isn't in transformation
and therefore
no form that's an essence.
'Matter, as such,'
Engels wrote, 'is the pure creation of thought ...
an abstraction';
matter only exists in particular forms.

So that these transient things, themselves, are what
    is Absolute;
these things
beneath the hand, and before the eye —
the wattle
lying on the wooden trestle,
pencils, some crockery,
books and papers, a river stone,
the dead flies and cobwebs
in the rusty gauze.

4

I am woken here when 'the sun gets to its feet
shouting'.
The sun takes a stride,
'wearing its waistband of human hair'.
I go out, over the morning's copious small water,
never touched,
and the golden breath covers the dense forest and the
    mountains,
the paddocks below
that are streaked with dead trees.

I walk down a long slope
where the bush is cut far back on either side;

the early sky, so light,
has a feeling of
the first day up again after illness;
the dew is dashed in the grass,
blue,
gold, red; as you pass above,
it lights up, everywhere you walk.

From this hillside
I can see, around a solid, wind-levelled, slant mass of trees,
the ocean —
like silver foil
that's been crumpled and smoothed again.

And below me, dark timber,
with those topmost cauliflower-clumps of eucalyptus
scattered, opaque,
against the ocean light.
Beyond, there are banana plantations
right along, over the billowing hillslopes,
and a few tin roofs
lit-up like dangling water-drops.
I hear, faintly, a dog yap,
and can see blue smoke
that is staggering along the air a little way.

I go further down;
wade a lagoon of whisky-coloured grass
onto the dirt road (soaked
to the knees), and pass
a deserted schoolhouse, with its red iron roof and tank,
and tennis court
lying within wire netting; and now a flock
of parakeets
sweeps by — it banks
on the morning, dark lift of wings — is settling
everywhere.

They're leaping about amongst the trees, and some dip
    into the court,
vague behind wire
as if flying through mist —
wheel up again
catching the sun — their feathers then
the colours of that dew. . . .

5

It was in China that men first could say
of this transitory world
it is Nirvana.

The Taoists had seen the universe in Self-Existent,
and that all particular things
spontaneously arise.

'If Heaven had produced its creatures on purpose
it would have taught them to love   (Wang Ch'ung)
and not to prey upon each other.

Rather, all things have come about through
    Transformation,
because they are one.
You do not find anything superior to things.'

Such a universe was spoken of as a Great Furnace
in which all that is
shall burn.

It is a fire that consumes the fire, undiminished.
How could Heaven have pity for that fate
its nature brings about?

'Though all is in destruction and regeneration at once
there is tranquillity in this disturbance.   (Chuang-tzu)
Tranquillity in disturbance is called Perfection.

There are ten thousand things being transformed,
and the sage is transformed along with them
without difference, without end.

Therefore, his movements are effortless as water;
his stillness, deep like a mirror;
his response, an echo.

His rarefied condition makes him seem to disappear.
He accepts his body with pleasure,
forgetting life and death.

To him there is nothing in the world that is greater
than the tip of a hair
that grows in spring.'

•

When something comes into existence
it is because of conditions that are favouring —

all-that-is, being interdependent,
combines to bring it forth,

and thus nature is good to man,
or at least, is more favourable than against him.

And everything appears, the Taoists said,
in dialectical relation —

it is like two stags
that lock horns close to the ground — a sound

of bamboos knocking together —
whose playful blood grows erect

in their veins: pushing
they manoeuvre

and stagger,
the dust arises

as all of these floating worlds.
On each world

and in every event of each
the same two stags contest.

And Lao-tzu, on leaving the Empire of Han,
at some vast age, to die —

riding on his buffalo
that was like a torrential rain —

wrote a poem to the people, and left it with the
      border guard:
that men should confess

it is the opposite of what we love
is good to us,

that it's only this weeping
which can make us glad.

●

The things of the earth
fill men with life
and swarm, like red corpuscles to a wound,
to do them good.
The earth feeds men aright;
the five grains are to feed them,
and the beans,
and the leaves for their soup;
and the water the same,
it goes down alive
inside men; and these fruits,
they feed men well.
And even Death —

the vinegar
that is found in the dish.
One ought to go out
into the forest and sun,
bathe in the streams and ocean,
and care for the body with oils
and comb the hair and decorate oneself
to sleep with another,
and join one's friends
in the grove of summer,
or beneath wide eaves
in dark weather, when the rain drips,
bringing wine.
And wander along the mountainside alone.
Because life is fleeting,
it is the breath of a bull in the wintry dusk.
Throwing away the self, 'let us hasten
to enjoy this life'.

6

The image of Buddha became a fat Chinaman
who was rolling on his haunches in a fallen-down robe,
twiddling as a fan
the end of a banana leaf,
with tits that wouldn't have looked out of place on a sow
and a laugh like a slice of watermelon —
to tear-up the conceptions of the mind.

Onto that way in harmony with nature there was joined
the sharp means of Release.
Before this, the Taoists were content with passivity,
and for discarding the self, most often
made do with wine.
The Emperor Wu-ti was first to hear the Unique Insight,
who asked of Bodhidharma,
define Buddhism.
Bodhidharma replied: Vast Emptiness.

•

Ma-chu got up onto the wood platform,
eased his legs in the Lotus,
laid aside his fan;
he started to trail smoking water on the green tea
    powder,
beating it with a whisk,
and looked over wet gravel, the heads of all the assembly,
between the darkness of wide, heavy doors,
to a lemon colour in the garden;
then he said to them, 'There is no Buddhahood for you
    to attain;
cling to nothing, that is the Tao',
and signalled for the crack
of the woodblocks together, for them to leave;
and sipped from the bowl, alone.

•

And there was a Master, Hsuan-chien,
told his students, after they'd sat in the courtyard for
    many days,
prostrating themselves, to be taken in,
'Pull on your clothes of a morning
and work along the hillside with the others,
or rake the leaves,
until you hear the dinner drum;
eat your meals,
and go to the john when you have to —
That's all.
There's no transmigration for you to fear, no
Nirvana to achieve.
Just respond to all things
without getting caught —
Don't even hold on to your Non-Seeking as right.
There is no other wisdom to attain.'

•

An afternoon rain
is drifting like sails of smoke
among these paperbark trees, about the shack;
it is the crumpling sound of cleaning up
cellophane wrap, close by,
and in one place, the green slap
of cow water.
'Sit straight, in Padmāsana, like a mountain,
keeping count of the breath, over and over,
so as not to touch your thought,
the eyes left open.'
You cannot dwell anywhere.
Realizing, beyond the intellect, that 'I' do not exist.

There is a soft, wet, vivid green,
a paddock, that rises
full as a breaker's first lifting,
now, after the cold steam;
and above it, struck by watery sun,
scaffolding tree-trunks, branch-beams, obliques, that
    shine
whitely, out of the black cumulus of bush.
And I hear rain tapping,
as if on canvas, from the guttering, and from where
a bird has skittered
all about this window, shaking the wet tree.

'A mind that's like a mirror,
in which things pass and leave no stain.'

7

I'm coming back with a haversack from the shop;
a beach resort
miles off,
walking all the way at the water's edge
along the empty sand.

Those shops they have forgot
to wind.

The one street, an old faded print,
squints in the glare;
outshone
by the plate-glass sea.

And I climb, one after the other, over
the headlands, on rock,
in late afternoon,

looking out to where all the clambering, wilted,
flaring

Ocean

begins, of a sudden, its bellowing and stamping,
the lowering of its shoulders,
a smoke-spray
blowing from them.

The surf comes in as though alive and tearing free
from under the net of foam —
making its break
with the panicky, bounding gallop of some great
    animal up
hopeless
onto the slippery shore.

And all the time along the horizon
those clouds,
that are like mountains with cliffs and valleys, now,
in the last, stretched-out sun —
that dreaming, far-off,
impossible land.

Night comes
quickly, over the water, as if water

flowing into the space left by the withdrawing sun,
and foam spreads
flatly all around me, phosphorescent,
bubbling and crackling in crab-holes in the sand.

The waves flicker
like a book left in some vast, empty house,
to a noise of doors slamming.

I am weary and cold, by now.
No one about.
Only, across the rising moon's long beam,
a bird flies,
skimming the horns of the sea.

This long beach,
beneath the immense imagery of night
and the night-bird's croak,
keeps on disappearing into the mist and dark.

And at such times, 'even in the mind of the enlightened
there arises sorrow',
so it's all right.

Telling the Beads

One drop is laid in each nasturtium leaf,
round as mercury,

and there are several on
every looped frond of the long flat grass;

these
clear sacs of plastic, tucked and full.

Plump, uncontained water,
precipitous,

held together by the air.
They are the most fragile particulars.

On grass that's loping everywhere,
in all the trajectories of a flea circus.

Thought balloons,
you infer

that I should fill each of you with its
apt word

which must be of a like transparency.
You are the mushrooms

conceived on the pure walls of the air;
anti-pebbles;

doodlings of a Botticellian elegance.
O *claritas,*

one thinks of lenses, floating upon each other,
dreamed by Spinoza

before a window full of sky,
all the Christians out of the house, and gone to church.

You are the digits of nature's prodigality.
You slip

on these stalks
as if one had become aware of the film

on strained eyes.
Presented on a febrifugal greenness —

someone who hadn't realized a need for refreshment
is made aware of an unventilated taste.

Looked at,
you offer hardly more than that.

This is authentic manna, it contains
no message and no promise,

only a momentary sustenance.
Run the drops from a stalk across your lip

they're lost
in the known juice of yourself, after the ungraspable

instant. Long-reputed but unresponsive
elixir.

Experiencing you, I see before me all the most refined
consolations of belief and thought.

Brushtail Possum

Thumps the water-tank
from out of the Gothic winter persimmon tree,
ticks like the start of rain
on tin
of the verandah
as we sit about after tea.

The banana leaves are shredded
like buckskin,
sway in night wind
against a closed window,
the fuel stove crackles,
the lamp-light an oily yellow.

We take some bread out:
a possum hung
over the sag of the guttering,
blackish-grey,
short-eared, snouted, anxious stare,
it swipes the bread with a human claw.

Eats it there;
nose pink and wet as a tongue,
tightly-packed fur
like moss. One eye is blue-white,
blind
from a twig or fight.

The whiskers wide-spread, like a spider's web.
The face twitching about
looks down
with its live eye
as with the one that's matching the moon,
against a salted sky.

Bellingen

bronze

linen tide

bronze

shadows

ibis

rowboat

farmlight

linen shadows

glide

Going Back, on a Hot Night

Now we are coming again towards a station;
out of the dark
countryside, the lights of a town,
beyond these sandy flats with their paperbark.

Over a hollow long metal bridge rumbles
the long train,
like a consignment of metal beer barrels
tumbled on concrete. And I see the small moon

above a dark sea, with the moonlight
in saucers, stacked-up,
teetering. Glimpsed as it reaches out
to mark the horizon. Now we almost stop;

creak forward. Street-light, palings. Archerville.
I know the Mail —
that I can stretch my legs a while
past these sacks and hampers, along the gravel.

I see a tea-leaf scrub, and the low moon again,
procession of one;
yellow kitchens; smoke; the pond-life of stars.
Through wide paddocks dart, like mice, a few cars.

I stand about. The frogs' hollow, ringing; regular
'clonk, clonk', from the scrub —
exactly the sound of a distant hammer
on framework. Going after some labouring job.

17 Poems

Waking at a station,
and across the blue-lit glass
this cold, far galaxy,
the rain.

The yachts — geese scattering
stately
in a flurry of harbour light.

A flag luxuriates:
those gestures of someone
taking a hot bath.

First daylight —
enough for the lacquer to hold
on the dresser top.

In a cheap hotel room
eating fruit —
it drips on the towel.

Across the level
eucalyptus forest, the sunlit
afternoon sea.

In a dark room
rustle of the long clothing
of the rain.

On the darkness
one star. An insect caught
in something, struggling.

Wake startled
in the afternoon —
heavy footsteps.
Kids bouncing
a soccer ball.

Small hotel, a morning of rain.
Reading in bed early
by soapy yellow electric light.

Signal box, somewhere;
a railway crossing sundown;
windy dunes. . . .

Alone, eating watermelon;
a back porch.
Seeds taken from
the lips, like hair.

The summer night,
a meandering wake
in waterlilies.

Wild, dark sea, and rain
falling. Through the lighthouse beam
a great bird flies.

Struggle to cut
a slice — now the pumpkin brays
like a mule.

Hot wind,
long boards of the verandah;
a bare rope clothesline
fluttering its hairs.

A long twilight,
milky-grey. Raindrops on the window,
gulls on the grass.

Reflection

Evenings, there are people with no intention of buying
who stop to look through the fish shop glass —
men with noses that are soaked full of alcohol,
old women who speak to the hand-led children that pass.

Water runs down these windows in clam-shell pattern.
Within, there's bounty, stainless fittings, clean light,
heaped prawns, and flounder white as ice cream,
the lairs' highway, the suburbs in their mangrove night.

Scotland, Visitation

North of Glasgow, the train wound like a kite's tail,
in the first spring weather,
under the clambering, close horizon —
that skyline, semaphore.
The brown grass, at the time, with such perfected
bright enamel
for the sky, reminding us of Australia:
of deeply-rolling, open country out from Kyogle;
except for the crooked
Japanese-scrawled, blackened pine trees,

instead of sparse eucalypts,
and a sudden tambourine-jangle of light through the beech
    leaves.
This after Glasgow, a place dull as Brisbane.
It is a landscape of great beauty, with small visual tradition —
even in Glasgow library
there seemed only two books of painting, both on
    Constructivism.
Yet, the Flemish blue of the lochs, like the Virgin's robe,
and the sudden, long hillsides
piebald in broken snow,
brilliant like a tropical sand.
Below the hills there were stiff, damp shadows,
pastel rocks, purplish-grey,
those red cattle that are like flood-wrack
hanging near stranded water,
and bulging low hills, bound down with stone walls like
    string.
We passed the upholstered sheep-lawns
reaching to a lawn-like sea,
and grey gables sleeping before a page of the Sound.
And then, neat English cars on the turf,
and the white lacquer and old stone of our ventilated sea
    town.
Like Richard Hannay,
we colonials were spoiled, for the spoiled southern home-
    country,
and had fled north. I walked all day
on the moor, alone,
with some genetic string plucked and vibrating within.
The only other moving thing,
except for a few sheep, that barely moved,
was the shadow of a bird, hung
different places on the grass —
although, in that bright sunlight, I could not find it above.
And just at dusk, there was a lone white bird, hurrying
in the distance
along dark water,

before the corroded facade of a pine forest.
So I turned back.
The black promontories, spiked and furry with trees,
drifted in the misty loch.
And it was then that I could see, beyond them, in the furthest uplands,
dark, brutal-shouldered forms
amongst a cauldron-smoke. . . .
I thought later of how, like children, men have done that
which is done to them. The apparent spirits
in the earth have taught us. Our fear,
and humiliation, bred hatred.
And yet the earth is Empty. It is innocent.
As everything, I thought, of that replete ground's cruel
history,
was, in some last consideration, innocent.

The Dusk

A kangaroo is standing up, and dwindling like a plant
with a single bud.
Fur combed into a crest
along the inside length of its body,
a bow-wave
under slanted light, out in the harbour.

And its fine unlined face is held on the cool air;
a face in which you feel
the small thrust-forward teeth lying in the lower jaw,
grass-stained and sharp.

Standing beyond a wire fence, in weeds,
against the bush that is like a wandering smoke.

Mushroom-coloured,

and its white chest, the underside of a growing mushroom,
in the last daylight.

The tail is trailing heavily as a lizard lying concealed.

It turns its head like a mannequin
toward the fibro shack,
and holds the forepaws
as though offering to have them bound.

An old man pauses on a dirt path in his vegetable garden,
where a cabbage moth puppet-leaps and jiggles wildly
in the cooling sunbeams,
the bucket still swinging in his hand.

And the kangaroo settles down, pronged,
then lifts itself
carefully, like a package passed over from both arms —

The now curved-up tail is rocking gently counterweight
    behind
as it flits hunched
amongst the stumps and scrub, into the dusk.

The Estates

We drive on back roads,
across the hessian-coloured paddocks that are packed with
        dust.
The shade is left here of a few trees
like sprinkled water.

The tallest thing, high-tension lines,
these ledger rulings, among which the small clouds bloom
and vanish, like idle thoughts.
The mountains behind, a broken wall in the haze of collapse.

Rejoin the highway, where the bush is flapping in tatters.
Billboards grow wild. One,
a great arrow of sheet metal, is sticking up
obliquely, with the Lurex message HOMES — TURN HERE.

A net of blank, wide-open avenues
has been thrown over these cleared undulations,
and wooden frameworks stand, riddled with a dry
        brilliance,
on orange clay, beside rotary clothes hoists.

Completed, the houses are split-level, with chequered roofs,
garage doors wide as billboards, wrought iron curlicues about
great flagstone patios,
cast-metal columns, and concrete flower-troughs by the drive.

Now whole estates present the planes
of their picture windows and serviette-shaped gables,
one beyond the other, garnished with shrubberies and
        pencil pines,
against what seems here Perspex blue.

Ostentation is the estates' ugliness —
they're like those drawn-out American cars, with the fins and
        chrome.
And next, the town appears; all this biscuit-coloured brick,
the expansive gesturing.

Streets hang open. The lighting is elegant as dental
     instruments.
Flicker of a few walkers, and of many plastic flags
over vast concrete
of the service stations. A pneumatic blast of sun.

Lifting on, like a speedboat, down the highway.
Beside us, the TV aerials seem to make a thin steam
above the packed shapes in caravan parks —
as if the people there are slowly boiling in their figuring.

And you notice, too, the floodmarks of each year on houses
     near the river,
in this or another town, into the twilight of motels.
So now, you see how we've failed,
and you're beyond those lies about what profit has done.

The Skylight

Dark Glasses

They lend a camera-lens intensity, and isolation,
in the sun-bathing heat,
to the blue hydrangeas across the lawn, whose each
    perfect dome
is made up
of unwavering jabs of mauve; and to a chipped laminate
cane stool, in between, that stands
palpable to sight
on the pencil-shaving grass.
The fence is coated with a small-leafed, dripping vine
like wallpaper:
each curlicue's edge
that sharply drawn. I turn my sight
on the equally sharp
definition of these potato chip scraps of bark
lifted on the grass,
above the tilt and scrabble
of ants, and feel myself trickle in the slowly
tightening press of the sun;
playing a breath-constricting, dangerous game.
The cicadas dilate and contract
as one, like fingers screeching down
plastic walls, in
crazy, rhythmic monotony. The sky
is an injection of maximum
blue, straight into the soul.
Supine, I prise myself up a little off the towel, to look
where she's standing at the hose,
beneath the verandah,
in the bottom of her bikini, drinking
and spraying at her daughter
behind the windows. She comes back cripple-
footed on the grass;
laughing and awry, so that water shakes either way
from her loose breasts, still white.
— I rotate my head down, a
few ratchets,

quickly, to see, above the dark glasses,
her breasts,
that are white as ice-cream
in her tan:
oiled and wet,
they look as though in syrup, or honey; each
    decorated
with a quince-coloured fruit.
And they feel,
I'd say, rather like
very fine, damp plastic bags do, when tightly packed
    with honey.

'In the early hours . . .'

In the early hours, I have come out to lean in the empty corridor of the train, as it's crashing and lurching through the night.

A liquefied dark scrub. And those paddocks where silverish-grey mist is rising, slowly as a stirred moon dust.

The orange moon, like a basketball fumbled over waste ground, is bouncing amongst the tops of a dark forest.

In the frosty, thick night a single farmhouse light floats wetly as a flare.

I have lain awake in such a bed, and it has seemed to me, also, it would be sufficient to be one of those carried within this wind-borne sound. . . .

(And I can remember, too, the mail train: a fine chain of lights as I stood in the paddocks of a wintry dusk. Its sound was that of wind through the swamp oaks.)

Motel Room

You keep on thinking of someone who woke here in the
    night,
lying still partly clothed amongst this bed,
when the television screen was a small animal, bundled-up,
shrill and squirming,
within a soiled white sheet;
and of how his mouth felt like a public place —
the phlegm, fumes and scraps
on the pavement of his tongue.
He couldn't remember which motel he was in —
the Sapphire, Blue Pacific, Palm Terrace, or Shangri-la.
The semi-trailers were meat-grinding
outside on the highway, as now;
getting down into the gristle and the bone
just here. He lifted himself, to wallow after the lavatory,
clothes twisted all over him,
and noticed how the things that he'd dropped everywhere
didn't change the look of no-one's place.
He made it back, onto the bed. Near this red lampshade
whisky left in its bottle
would have looked like petrol. And he raised his head,
again, to feel about
through the coverlet, and to sniff at this chewing-gum
wad of pillow — and fell back,
relieved if he could remember
at least there hadn't been a girl in here, that night.

On Contradictions

The black swan, drifting,
suggests a cartoon
about a Victorian lady,

being all refinement and propriety, with
a bustle.
Yet, on land,

it is at once a lurching
tough — the whole body
like shoulders;

it keeps doubling back,
then stretching-out, flexing,
the threatening

length of neck;
its mussel-shell beak, clacking,
drips;

a leathery
slap on the stones,
and hissing.

But it leaves
along the water, and now
again

is calm as a paddle-
wheeler, on some idle
pleasure course.

With millinery's most extravagant
bouquet —
the tail-feathers,

that are each curled inwards
fluffily
from the sides.

These live feathers have all
the ashen colour,
the tremor, and frailty,

of layers of a newspaper
burning
in a daylight clear flame.

Walking in an American Wood

The moist deer woods seem sliding down, on one side of the
    railway line;
on the other, the slate Ohio; and beyond,
continuous factories, black and hieroglyphic-square,
through a feather-brushed drizzle, at dawn.
From the long nozzles of those recurrent chimneys is torn,
in bursts, a heavy vermilion flame,
rolling sideways, heavily as lava,
and the grey sky beats and crumples there, as though a
    pounded drum.

The eye of Osiris, where a bough is missing,
on the tooled leather of a silver birch, as I turn into the
    woods, before
a stack of dead cars,
and old houses on the outskirts of town, maple-splattered.
The pretence at innocence of an American architecture:
child-drawn, blocky, in clapboard, with wide-eyed windows,
    and simple steep roof.
Cars, long as crocodiles, are slewed up and sleeping, as yet,

on the bank before each door, and the television aerials
   are packed together
like waiting cattle-prods.
There is no more innocence here
than there's sincerity in all of that talk about you're
   welcome and having a nice day.
Americans seem to believe you may have to eat or be
   eaten, and therefore
the complementary, frightened insistence on sociability.
I can make out a bike tube and cardboard boxes flung into
   the branches
above someone's yard, and wet newspaper and bits of
   automobile lying about.
In another yard, a half-sized statue of Jesus,
with downward, open arms, is looking towards the house;
and, as always, an American flag, big as a double
   bed-sheet;
this one on a pole from an upstairs window.

Inside the woods there are stiff little ferns, coffee-dusted
   with spore,
all about the steep, leaf-mulch ground. I climb through
   fallen sticks.
Left-over snow lies between roots and behind large rocks,
   as if heaps of wet salt.
From the hilltop, I look back, among trunks, onto the
   river,
that's moving like poured treacle,
the flat folds of its pouring shown-up by sideways light.
The mist is rising eerily as a flying saucer, from the
   further, river-bound woodland.

I walk on, going downhill a long way. Branches slant right
   to the ground, like eaves
with many slates missing, making irregular, crooked, long
   openings.

Rising steam all through these sodden woods, and
    occasional lime-coloured lit undergrowth.
Sometimes I see another ridge, across the valley; the pine
    trees there each the shape of a pine cone.
Mostly, all the dimensions are starred with leaves.

The slope levelling out, I climb over rocks, in the open,
toward a few older pines. These are an almost upright volley
    of spears
landed together. Or they could seem abandoned teepee poles,
with some dangling feathers, in a slow wet smoke.
There are long projections drawn against their straight edges
through the sunlit mist. I sit to watch
the light that's coming around them grow, burning away at
    one side of this overlapping stand.

Then, further on, black trunks against the lake — their long
    dry laterals whiskered like tap roots.
I come to the brown sand of the shore.
The little matted sticks and stranded froth remind me of a
    cocoon.
Along the open ground is old snow, the palest mauve, strewn
    thinly as fertiliser.
A cold watery breath climbs
through the air and through the bones of one's head;
it is refined into light, fleeing upwards, becoming frailer
    and frailer.
The lake's glare and insubstantiality are dissatisfying,
throughout the face, and in the throat, and the body. . . .
I don't really know why I've come here, looking outwards
    into light,
nor do I bother to remember, but it feels now as though
    something that's in me
will have to keep onward in this way, going barefooted
    through the stars.

Travels en Famille

She began at once to use the train compartment
as though it were a room at home —
we'd arrived in our hammered, canine furs,
along the platform, through the rain,

and she hung the child's bright socks,
our overcoats and scarves on anything
that seemed a hook. With her best smile
which stayed there, like a transfer.

Two old women, under rugs, were cackling
their uncertainty. The man was cornered
behind a newspaper like a dented visor.
She dried the child's feet on her tartan skirt.

How 'embarrassing'. — I could peel open a book,
as usual. Schoolgirls were grinning through
a glass partition over the women's heads;
they tried their winking on me, and then wrote

something in fog along windows of the corridor
to squeal about, and at once rub off
for one another, aghast. The train jerked
as if given a great kick, and started running

almost at once above an open countryside.
A photograph of assorted river gravel
montaged on one of sodden, moss-bright fields.
Everything creaked like a soldier's gaiters.

The electric light, warm butter; and our coats
stirring thickly around in their steam.
She read out the child's story, and we all laughed.
Beside us, a wall in two equal shades —

the dim green earth, and a mauve-grey sky.
A few trees at the fields' edge, as on a shelf,
like old pieces of steel *art nouveau*; their foliage
the shapes of Japanese fans. I thought

A perfect moment, but then forgot about it.
We came to a small, flat town lying in the rain
and through its empty streets a sunset light appeared
shining on the sides of wet wooden houses.

Smoke

As if through a slanted blind,
the sun is made shafts among the immense rungs
of a Moreton Bay fig —
it comes sliding between that Gaudi-like, visceral
    architecture;
a slow,
egg-thickened, steamy
mixture, precisely-sliced and,
in rows, gently conveyor-belted down.
I watch across a road of
cattle-race traffic, and above the wall.

Over there, a gardener is at work:
his leaf-smoke
only visible within the slatted sun.
Discontinuously, smoke rises
and rears back, slides downward along itself, and winds
about, is gathered-up again, swelling into vast Chinese
    dragon sinuosities.
And, calmly, it seems giving birth; it keeps wavering and
    shredding,
then remerging, within the one great shape, like Taoist
    water symbology —
above all the interpenetrating, harsh lunging past here.

I'm waiting around beside a shopwindow's deep pool;

looking in sideways, I watch the people —
the threshings and winnowings of the city —
come right up and pass me blindly; leading with their faces
into their lives.
By turning to either side, I see
in the panels of sunlight across the way, or in this glass,
either the eternal process, as it has been stylised and
    revealed,
or its particulars,
that are like smoke.

The Canoe

a pod
for the hand

is the canoe in
the mind

like a hammock
this dialectic

of the soporific
and cautious

it is tandem skiing
but we

are launched
trees

fallen in the river
steep

from the bank
steeping

the dawn's
grey weather

in the black boughs
bits

of pink and lemon
brightening

like watered
sherbet

the tide
is tightly stretched

a first
sunlit passage

the bees
of day

the curled leaves
are carried

high
and lightly

processional
into deep shade

silence
the whip bird's

long
smoothly-peeled

call
that breaks off

wetly
a green

overhang
and the high-lifted

twigs
and dust

membranous
water

now the river's
a sunlit

empty plaza
on the far shore

the tree-line
is burned away

by glare
a forest highway

and we
lone refugees

with
a perambulator

cobalt sky
the bush

like overgrown weeds
high banks

of orange clay
a folded

duck's body
gliding

duck-breasted
swivel

the forest slopes
built

of stacked-up
tree clumps

dead trees
scratches

down the mountain-face
on a smoky dark

glassiness
and the river drops

downhill of a sudden
takes

rotored flight
straps tight

the chest
a wild bumping

aeroplane
but with lots of

shoving off
off

off
we try

and then running out on
roller-skates

to
go creeping across

the sleeping
dark

under cliffs
in the crow-calling

silence
of late afternoon

a grey
marshland

where the river gives
itself away

before the high
long silver

of the sea
and the backyards

along these slopes
with their wash

flying
a rusted chassis on

a mud bank
the mangroves

collapsed
footballers' scrum

in blue mud
and

caravan parks dogs
kids yelling

we land in
the estuary

a small town's
marina

and walk through
summer dust

paddocks
above the sea

into town
to a restaurant table

in the dusk
watching

the lights of the ships
going by

The Sea-Shell

White as crockery,
it stands on the ledge of the long verandah window
in a white plank wall.

The trellis-lights —
negative, scrap shapes — are swung in here stiffly
as torch beams.

The shell is a lifting spinnaker.
And close-up, there are patterns in beige,
similar to a feather's.

The shell is wound
the same as pastry, and it has the same decorative
ruffled edging.

Coloured lead inserts in these bare windows.
Vine-patterns are stirring. Conifers,
bird movements. A Sunday.

The sound in the shell
is that of the whole Order at their evening meal,
along dim passages, behind doors.

The shell is cool, remote;
its shape causes a peristalsis in your palm,
it is breast-tipped.

Closed, adamant shell —
you think of some girl, who has been waited for here;
who's come, at last, from church;

who is received in her cool,
coiffured whiteness. Like the shell,
underneath her that dark passage, and damp smell.

'The best place ...'

The best place to watch the rain
is from the window of an apartment building,
on the third floor,
looking across an empty sports field, at night.
Someone should have left those tall sodium lights on,
faintly lighting the rugby goals, in a real storm.
And there should be taller buildings about

with a few of their orange and yellow windows still burning,
balanced on blackness, in asymmetrical pattern.
By this light you'll see,
caught in a long drawn-out pleasure, the vast collapse
and sifting away of a whole mountain-stack
of new slippery straw —
the bleached silver, and frail pliant gold,
whirling off.
Or the rain is a headful of blond, loose hair
struck by wind,
flaring out, and drawn upon — as stirring as if
that's actually what you saw.
Growing heavier, the rain can seem not a rushing down at all,
in some lit places,
but a rapid oscillation, a flicker,
maintaining itself in mid-air.
The night as filled with rain as a plank with splinters.
Eventually, you turn inside, the long window left bared its
    full length,
and on a table is the typewriter, and the sawn block of white
    paper,
one sheet a curving grass-blade.
To the side in this room, in a smaller but similarly brazen
    window,
a tree-top is plastering,
thumping, and twisting itself about, like some enthusiastic
    postal clerk.
You sit down to the pleasure of writing when there is
    nothing that has to be written —
no article or review required; no editor
makes his pills ineffectual tonight
by chewing them with your name.
The desk lamp
curves its shadow across
all the shelved books, and they become
a crowd canopied in that vast South American football
    stadium,
whose voices now, in the midst of play,
you can no longer hear.

You're alone, the night before you.
The rain overwhelms itself outside. It is happiness.

Bondi

The waves are a shoal of white fins, in the end of every
    downhill street,
and along the streets are stacked blunt-faced blocks of
    flats:
big, plastery, peeling buildings, in cream, with art deco
    curves and angles.
Behind this, for a thousand acres, the buckled suburbs of
    dark brick.
Curtains trail outwards on the heat, and a smell of gas
    leaks,
above singed grass in tiny yards, grey palings, chlorine-
    blue hydrangeas,
gas pipes like creepers over walls.
There are garbage bins left lying about, empty milk
    bottles on marble steps,
always snail-dribble across the concrete, to the crushed
    snail shells.
The sun trundles around and around, amongst its
    flapping fire.
In the longest street, out toward the cave-in of the
    head-land, is a children's park,
where, through empty swings, with their oversized hot
    chains, the surf swings.
Out here are callow home units of pale brick, fenestrated
    as that rock face
below the cliff's edge they're built upon.
Beyond a last railing, the sea throws over and spreads its
    crocheted cloth
across the rock table, and (something you can't watch for
    long — it is like madness)
draws it off once again.
Around at the beach-front, rattling fun parlours, discos,
    and milk-bars, the sign-painting

lurid as tattoos, thickly over them.

Cars are tilted along all the gutters, strung together closely as
    caterpillars,

in the colours of children's sweets. The grit settles, coating
windscreens and duco; vinyl seats bake in the sun,

and that smell will sicken the overwrought children in the
    late afternoon, going home.

All day these headlands lie spread apart to the pleasurable,
    treacherous elements.

The place seems scoured by weather of every other ideal.

But then, a white yacht will appear in the ultramarine
    passage, an icon

of perfect adaptation, and the people along the sand,

as though in a grandstand, or those wading out

through the low waves towards it, seem all of them every-
    where over this

like walking moths, that fan its easy passage with their wings.

It goes wandering on midway in the spectrum of blue before
    them, in the garment of serenity.

This is the only sort of vision we shall have, and it costs
    money,

and therefore Bondi is lying crammed together, obtuse, with
    barely a tree, behind us —

Every cent is firstly for the secure mechanisms of comfort.

It is not pleasure, to be exact, but its appropriation. And not
    mindlessness, but the mind.

For at the beach, so much that is nature can be seen to have
    been called

into the one procession of decay. Flesh become crude and
    brief

as figures shaped out of beach sand. So many of these people
look as though used like Bondi grit, with its scraps and butts
    and matchsticks.

Still, the young girls are loping on the sea-front, who secretly
amaze themselves with an easy skill they've found —

who can swing their breasts and all the shapes that are
    surging on their bodies

as if the drum majorettes for this parade.

At dusk, the parking spaces above the sea have emptied
and sand blows along the bitumen like smoke.
The garbage bins on posts are steep in their slipping litter.
And the gulls, that run and screech and scatter each other
    amongst it, never make
contented noises — are scrabbling constantly;
only sometimes one of them is carried off by the wind,
    down the bay, and it goes along
on its outriggers, smoothly; beautiful, particularly in the
    dusk,
when it flows away as smoothly, sideways, as the
    running shallows —
its whiteness, that is picked up by the whiteness of a
    wave's single wingbeat,
out there on the deep mauve water, creating a vast space.

The Poem

The paddocks there are so wide open
she says you always feel
that the lid has been left off everything.
It's all gone hard and stale.

The children have to stay in the shade;
they hang from the verandah,
and the game they fight about is discovering
a demand upon her.

On the backs of her hands, in this light, open
small, dry screams.
She is bringing in the sunlit bed-clothes,
putting together the seams.

Sheets still pegged she takes into her fist,
and stands inhaling each one:
taut with air, white as a heron in the moonlight.
This, which she has done.

A Country Town

It was the sort of town where there is always an empty
    block of land
on the main street.
I was there one Sunday in autumn
and I saw through this gap how the afternoon above the
    hills was growing white
and was broken with swallows, insect-dancing.
Above that, the light had become white burgundy, and
    above that, all at once, indigo
and waiting for the first damp star.
The deep block where I stood was fenced with rusty,
    freehand lines of wire
and carried some old foundations,
hoops of thorny vine bowled in among them,
and a concrete slab, that had once been the bathroom
    floor, now littered with finely-broken bottles.
Down at the back there was wood-smoke, above the
    galvanised roofs of another street,
and a few bare willows, in a tangle
like untidy basket work.
I watched a cow grazing in the shadows, on spongy
    mounds of grass,
an old bathtub tilted for its water trough.
This block was almost at one end in a street of deep
    awnings; at the other was the pub,
where local workmen, all timber-getters, sat
giving nothing away to each other, the loved undulation
    of a glass
felt by the cleft at the end of each arm, for hour after hour.
I'd listened a while, then come outside with my drink,
    into the freshly peeled twilight,
to the sound of a car, a dog's bark,
the shouts of a few kids
who pedalled in great bounds, beneath the level of their
    bike seats,
circling when the street became a road again.
A flying fox twitched overhead

like something caught alive on a stick (a country
    pleasure); and some midges
were moving together,
bouncing up and down, left and right, a bit ragged
but always in formation, as though being shaken around
    inside an invisible box.
I turned to the empty block, then,
and noticed in the last of the daylight a crooked tap
within a surge of grass, almost secretive, and the way it
    kept dripping
fast — unreasonably fast.
I was staring, as if through a keyhole.
That tap seemed frightening, and indecent, having gone
    on how long unnoticed there, dripping fast,
fast, yet silently,
with a hammer's little finalizing silver blows.

Sketch of the Harbour

The long, wet trajectory of the ferry's railing
widely outswinging
is safely caught in my hand.

And I watch a yacht that is coasting by,
at its bow the fuming
of a champagne bottle's lip.

All about on the harbour the yachts are slowly waltzing,
or in close-up
their ecstatic geometry.

Light fragments crackling above the suburbs and water,
whitely, as from a welder's torch,
on a soap-white day.

In the shadow of the ferry, the oily, dense water
is flexile, striated
as launching muscles.

But further out, there is only sunlight over a surface —
a constant flickering, like a lit-up
airport control.

And the gulls, white as flying foam, lie beside us here
with the clear balloons of air
underneath their arms.

Emptying the Desk

Lastly, in the bottom drawer, a packet.
He breaks it open. And everything there feels the same as
    ever.
This had been the first time for him.
He recalls standing in that house, in mouldy darkness.
Rain collapsed outside
like a hurled net, the trees slashing and struggling
    underneath it.
His torch-beam, about the room,
was a trapped swallow.
He had hauled back the curtains, taking hold of their
    heavy moth fur.
No sign, that night, of the distant lit suburbs.
Dead flies along the window-sill, and hung inside an
    open jar.
And rain went on rushing smoothly into the earth
through one street light
the way the gleaming sides of an express train enter
    a tunnel.
He sees again the fence-eating grass,
and, like smoke drifting, a single car
that passed in the road.
There were some hobo's dirty blankets on a mattress, in
    one corner,
trodden against the wall;
a deal table, stained and burned; two overturned
    aluminium chairs;
newspaper everywhere. There was glass underfoot

from a broken-up, heavy sideboard.
He'd moved to the next room, stepping
along a slippery path. And in there, his torch-beam
    fell, almost at once,
on someone's eyes. It leapt, like a scorched finger.
He forced it back. His heart had stabbed downward
    through his bowels.
The torch-beam, he remembers, trembled
as if it were a water-light reflected indoors.
It was someone plainly dead.
And dried blood was everywhere, the way that vandals
    smear their shit about.
She wore some scrap of underwear,
and was like candle-wax; so delicate.
He has probably never, he realises, for a whole day
    since then,
quite forgotten her.
Her feet were rolled open in a clown's walk,
her arms held downwards in the way
those young girls dance.
The blood, that made crazing all over her face,
was sticking underneath her head.
She'd seemed like porcelain — a shattered figurine,
    with an expression
horrified by what had happened to itself.
All this was a long time ago.
In some of these photographs white circles are drawn;
in others, the shape of her body has been traced on
    the dirty floor.
No more since then. He's often imagined
a motel room somewhere; 3 a.m.; rain dripping in
    the alley;
someone propped above her,
his brain haemorrhaging its pleasure. A need going on.
All these years, that her feet have only been running in
    a few scraps of heather;
and her mouth long since has been forced open
by the root of some decorous tree.

Outside, a summer afternoon.
The secretaries are coming back from lunch, along
    the drive,
or are sitting on the grass together.
In a corner, between two wings of the building,
there are a few nondescript small bushes, each of them
    only leaves,
and these are stirring slightly, on the end of the light.

15 Poems

The curtains blowing
open, a sock stretched apart,
wide meadows.

Following a van up
a winding forest road. Swallows
flit between us.

Darkness, lake-hush;
a rowboat, allowed to drift, bumps
the starlight.

As if the sun
out of boredom has doodled weeds ...
a backyard.

This moon, the last
tilted sauterne, in a glass
that's fire-lit.

A definition
of art deco: in black and cream
the butterfly.

Boiling water
poured from a saucepan

into a water-bottle's neck.
On the edge of your mind
the waves fall.

Wintry sunlight;
the dry, plastery legs of a woman
in tennis skirt.

Dark bedroom. Listening
to a rain-wet tree — its lovely
negligence.

Homesick for Australia,
a dream of rusty Holdens
in sunlit forests by the highway.

A cathedral interior —
these long tapers of rain lighting
candles on the twilit river.

Staved-in, the old rowboat
we had as kids
has foundered this last time
in a field of grass.

Wire coat-hangers,
misshapen, in a hotel wardrobe.
Steamy afternoon sun.

Cold swimming pool,
plastic blue. A bare tree's reflection,
its roots x-rayed.

Two magpies stepping
on the verandah. A ploughed hillside,
smoke, and cumulus.

A Day at Bellingen

I come rowing back on the mauve creek, and there's a
    daylight moon
among the shabby trees,
above the scratchy swamp oaks
and through the wrecked houses of the paperbarks;
a half moon
drifting up beside me like a jelly fish.
Now the reflected shapes are fading in the darkened
    rooms of the water.
And the water becomes, momentarily, white —
    magnesium burning.
My oars
have paused, held in their hailing
stance —
are melting;
and all the long water is a dove-grey rippled sand.
A dark bird hurries
low in a straight line silently overhead.
The navy-blue air, with faint underlighting,
has a gauze veil hung up within it, or a moist fresh
    smoke.
I land in the bottom of an empty paddock,
at a dark palisade
of saplings.
Among the ferns, dead leaves, fresh leaves, dry lightning-
    shaped twigs,
a cold breeze
comes up, rattling shreds all around.
A wind-blown star
is being drawn forth like a distant note.
The house I am the soul of lies,
hollow, on a ridge across the paddocks, although long
    occupied already
by the scouts of night.
I drag up the rowing boat, its rusty water slopping,
and start off, loosely in boots,
across the spongy, frog-bubbling undulations

of these coarse-bitten flats,
in a sharpened cow-dung smell.
After a day of sitting about,
spent reading and scribbling on margins
or bits of windy paper, and in remembrances,
the hours of which have passed
the way that water-drops fill at the downwards tip
of a twig,
I took the rowing boat out.
Rowed miles,
into the river, and downstream, over an ale-coloured
    brackishness —
through the societies of midges, in their visual uproar
(bronze-lit, like Caesar come to the Forum),
right out, equidistant from shore;
saw the birds swing on long trapezes across the green
    alcoves;
and followed all the notations of the tree-line
to those at dusk like flaking rust.
I came back with the slow-motion strides of a water
    spider over fluttered water.
As always, it has worked.
Now the mind is turned down, like a gas flame
in a dark kitchen,
where the wind and all the night sounds can again be
    heard.
It lies once more beneath the truth of the body.
All of my demanding
has become, crossing these paddocks, and watching
    the other stars appear,
as delicate as the first mould
on black bread, simply to take an axe and go on
up to the end of the cleared land, underneath the
    hooded eucalyptus forest,
to crack some firewood
from a weather-tightened grey log,
for a hot, deep bath, that I can draw out through
    the evening.

Landscape

After the tide's long gear-shifting gesture,
glimpsed among the bush,
climbing down toward ocean shallows'
tilting opalescence.

A washed sandbar, the yellow of a melon;
rocks' wet terracotta;
a viridescent cloud,
sponge-pitted, that is crinkled weeds —

these are somewhere underneath the sluice
of cellophane-clear,
fast-drawn-off-the-roller, billowing
water, light-glistened.

Leaning above this, out of rock, angophoras —
flesh-pink clamber
all over the dense, ink blueness of the sky.
Trees like Schiele's posturings.

And two of them clash, their shadows clamped on
a single stone — leaping for the sun
with fingertips
that basketball players try to grow.

Bringing the Cattle

All afternoon I've lain about in this illuminated country, on one of the round hillsides, and have heard the squeak of cropped grass, and smelt the cow smell, like a warm convalescence, the cows close and oblivious, or with a sun-drugged interest.

A hare stopped in the heat, and shivered, folding back its ears — the same way as the butterfly did its wings, on a plaited head of grass that hung above the ripe valley.

But now the farmer, who all year wears shorts and rubber boots, and wades through the running shallows of paddock grass, who cracks his cattle with a stick across their bony out-crops, makes his voice float here.

And the cows jolt down with everything swinging — the bellies, rounded as hammocks stretched full, and the four long teats, on udders that are grooved and furry like a peach.

Their foreheads, between the big eyeballs' slow permanent surprise, make a wide, hollow-sounding target for the crowbar-wielding farmer when they've something broken or a germ.

The hips, draped sharp Henry Moore shapes. And the splayed feet are placed with mincing care, as if they've high heels on.

Now a last cow is flouncing along the top of the slope, its spider-web fine thread of slobber blown out long in the final brightness of the sun.

The air is staining quickly with moisture, and the paddocks fill with vacancy.

These corridors lain across the beaten grass are alight and chill. The river, willow-shouldered, that was silk in the distance, now at twilight is all ice panels.

And the mist that will lie kerosene-blue and thick as smoke, through the night an incubus on creeks and dams, and that will drag among the raided, fluttering cornstalks, and stick the turned earth thickly, is already starting to seep from every dark socket of the ground.

So, following the cattle, and at their pace, I am also going down.

Karl Marx

Karl Marx was playing a parlour game
with his daughters. To their question
What is the quality one should most abhor?
he wrote: Servility.

This was found — a scrap of paper
amongst the family albums and letters;
it is the most essential of all
the Complete Works.

Watching by the Harbour

There is a late Sunday over the leaf-smoke suburbs.
The sidling of a candle snuffed
sets forth
above the burred metal plate of the bay.

And that smoke quickly becomes as frail and failing
in the strength of wintry light
as Oates
walking out alone into Antarctica.

Now the sky has paled like a butcher's clean shirt.
Far beneath it, a spread seagull
idly tries
its segments of a compass inscription.

Afternoon seems light that's escaping beneath a door.
In a cooling breeze the water shrivels
the same as flesh —
It happens mostly on the surface of the mind.

The plaster-thick paint of an end wall, in that hillside,
is gold-leafed, a moment, among
makeshift eucalypts.
Cattle-tracks of clear light trodden on the water.

At this reserve, the deep shadow of a ligamented fig,
a tilted lawn, the harbour set with sails
like restaurant tables.
Now early lights come out, smoky as lanterns.

'O time too swift, O swiftness never ceasing.' — This world,
it seems, is rattling in a gypsy's
hands, that part
and reveal how the things we love have gone.

The hills shall be valleys, and the valleys will be hills.
And someone who could drag open
a bow, in youth,
has fired away his life, lost with the arrow.

Fully dark; lit by distant hordes. And along the foreshores
you see now where there is nailed
a human warmth.
Our bivouac's encircled, in mountainous night.

Diptych

1

My mother told me how one night, as would often
        happen, she'd stayed awake
in our weatherboard house, at the end of the dark,
        leaf-mulched drive,
waiting for my father, after the pubs had closed,
knowing he would have to walk
miles, 'in his state',
if no one dropped him home

(since, long before this, he had driven his own car off a
    mountain-side,
and, becoming legend, had rode
on the knocked-down banana palms
of a plantation, right to the foot, and someone's door,
the car reared high on a great raft of mutilated,
    sap-oozing fibre,
from which he'd climbed down, unharmed, his most soberly
    polite,
and never driven again).
This other night, my mother was reluctant to go out, and
    leave us kids asleep,
and fell asleep herself, clothed, on the unopened bed,
but leapt upright, sometime later, with the foulest taste —
glimpsed at once
he was still not there — and rushed out, gagging,
to find that, asleep, she'd bitten off the tail
of a small lizard, dragged through her lips. That bitterness
    (I used to imagine),
running onto the verandah to spit,
and standing there, spat dry, seeing across the silent,
    frosty bush
the distant lights of town had died.

And yet my mother never ceased from what philosophers
    invoke, from 'extending care',
though she'd only ever read the *Women's Weekly*,
and although she could be 'damned impossible' through a
    few meal-times, of course.
This care for things, I see, was her one real companion in
    those years.
It was as though there were two of her,
a harassed person, and a calm, that saw what needed to
    be done, and
seemed to step through her, again.
Her care you could watch reappear like the edge of tidal water
in salt flats, about everything.
It was this made her drive out the neighbour's bull from our
    garden with a broom,

when she saw it trample her seedlings —
back, step by step, she forced it, through the broken
    fence,
it bellowing and hooking either side sharply at her all
    the way, and I
five years old on the back steps calling
'Let it have a few old bloody flowers, Mum.'
No. She locked the broom handle straight-armed across
    its nose
and was pushed right back herself, quickly, across the
    yard. She
ducked behind some tomato stakes,
and beat it with the handle, all over that deep hollow-
    ness of the muzzle,
poked with the millet at its eyes,
and had her way, drove it out bellowing; while I, in
    torment,
stood slapping into the steps, the rail, with an ironing
    cord,
or suddenly rushed down there, and was quelled, also,
repelled to the bottom step, barracking. And all,
I saw, for those little flimsy leaves
she fell to at once, small as mouse prints, amongst the
    chopped-up loam.

2

Whereas, my father only seemed to care that he would
    never appear a drunkard
while ever his shoes were clean.
A drunkard he would define as someone who had
    forgotten the *mannerisms*
of a gentleman. The gentleman, after all, is only known,
only exists, through manner. He himself had the most
    perfect manners,
of a kind. I can imagine no one
with a manner more easily, and coolly, precise. With
    him,
manner had subsumed all of feeling. To brush and dent
    the hat

which one would doff, or to look about, over each of us, and
    then unfold a napkin
to allow the meal, in that town where probably all of the
    men
sat to eat of a hot evening without a shirt,
was his passion. After all, he was a university man
(although ungraduated), something more rare then. My
    father, I see, was hopelessly melancholic —
the position of those wary
small eyes, and thin lips, on the long-boned face,
proclaimed the bitterness of every pleasure, except those of
    form.
He often drank alone
at the RSL club, and had been known to wear a carefully-
    considered tie
to get drunk in the sandhills, watching the sea.
When he was ill and was at home at night, I would look into
    his bedroom,
at one end of a gauzed verandah,
from around the door and a little behind him,
and see his frighteningly high-domed skull under the
    lamp-light, as he read
in a curdle of cigarette smoke.
Light shone through wire mesh onto the packed hydrangea-
    heads,
and on the great ragged mass of insects, like bees over a
    comb, that crawled tethered
and ignored right beside him. He seemed content, at these
    times,
as though he'd done all that he could to himself,
and had been forced, objectively, to give up.
He liked his bland ulcer-patient food
and the big heap of library books I had brought. (My
    instructions always were:
'Nothing whingeing. Nothing by New York Jews;
nothing by women, especially the French; nothing
translated from the Russian.')
And yet, the only time I actually heard him say that he'd
    enjoyed anything

was when he spoke of the bush, once. 'Up in those hills,'
he advised me, pointing around, 'when the sun is coming
    out of the sea, standing amongst
that high timber, you can feel at peace.'
I was impressed. He asked me, another time, that when
    he died
I should take his ashes somewhere, and not put him with
    the locals, in the cemetery.
I went up to one of the hills he had named
years earlier, at the time of day he had spoken of, when
    the half-risen sun
was as strongly-spiked as that one
on his Infantry badge,
and I scattered him there, utterly reduced at last,
    amongst the wet, breeze-woven grass.
For all his callousness to my mother, I had long
    accepted him.
After all, he'd given, or shown me, the best advice,
and had left me alone. And I'd come by then to think
    that all of us are pathetic.
Opening his plastic, brick-sized box, that morning,
my pocket-knife slid
sideways and pierced my hand — and so I dug with
    that one
into his ashes, which I found were like a mauvish-grey
    marble dust,
and felt that I needn't think of anything else to say.

Aubade

The cold night that was clamped on the land
falls loose, an unwound
vise, and is lifted off.

Light rises on the spider's web,
the way that a needle-drawn thread
is pulled through, to arm's length.

The room is a bush clearing,
a bale of light. A professional's grooming
these curtains, as in their youth.

And your long bright hair is like
the first paint-loaded brush stroke
that wanders before me over the white cloth.

Memories of the Coast

There would often be times when there was no life in the
    main street of a weekday,
and the road, going on, dipped beneath the sea;
a wind moving along the water, as though it were among
    grass tips,
beyond tarry telegraph wires, and the shoals and flat sheen
    of the bitumen.
We kids would come up from the beach onto four o'clock
    footpath heat —
hobbling barefoot and fast between awnings,
with our seawater towels, sand-chafing floppy shorts, zinc
    cream, spiked hair;
three or four of us, and dog — counting change,
once more, by the milkbar window's bleached posters,
    dead flies.
A brick side wall had a Bushell's sign more deeply blue than
    the sky.

On the way up, we came underneath a high paling
        fence, overhung with paspalum heads,
along a pathway of squeaking, flat-footed sand,
past some backyards — their woodpiles, cardboard
        boxes, lavatories,
long weeds, wide underwear —
and off to the other side, a black railway goods yard;
coming out onto shop fronts, that always looked half-
        witted, with their sun-in-the-eyes squint.
How poignant used to seem to me the beautiful,
        one-handed lady mannequin.
She was among bolts of cloth as big as papyrus rolls
        seemed on Sunday school cards.
We went reverently indoors, at Papandreou's —
to long floorboards, dusty air, the ice-cream scoops in
        a jar of milky water,
a dried shark's jaw,
flypaper so thickly used it was like a necklace of
        apple-pips,
chairs stacked on tables;
to a fifty year old bristled man who came chewing from
        out the back, the woman's side of it cut short,
for a threepenny-ha'penny sale.

At that time, there were only a few fibro weekenders
        around, off among the sandhills' fluttered grass,
with watertanks on damp-rotted stands, flyscreens
        hung askew,
a rusty dog-chain stretched toward a puddle.
Behind those places, the slant, low trees seemed fused
        in a solid black clump,
coarse-leafed and sapless;
and when we came out from playing our games there,
        all through that sandy, speckled bush,
onto blue metal and dust at the level crossing,
we'd always see a few Aboriginals
going with a bottle to the sandhills, on flat pod feet.

Beyond the railway line, the one hotel's high verandah stood
    on insect legs, above the emollient of a pavement
that was constantly hosed, shifting dogs.
In the early fifties, most houses of town were sown loosely
    along the first few hillslopes
(before the mountains, that moved through every blue tone
    of iris petal,
back within the land's smoulder, that reversed sea-spray).
The dusty streets had mainly weatherboard places
on low stilts; no pavement or kerbs, but each bungalow with
    its concrete front path,
and silvered steep roofing iron,
and rhubarb in the backyard.
At St John's, there'd often be a heifer browsing, biblically,
just outdoors from the baptismal font;
and inside, someone had told me once, there was a fisherman
    laid out, all his flesh
green-bearded with dangling prawns.
Most houses then looked over the shops, and the ply-mill
    smoke; over the muscle-building
bend of the Coast railway line;
the tiles of the school; the listless rugby goalposts, near
    grassy sandhills;
the afternoon drizzle on the ziggurats
of peeled eucalyptus poles;
the Melanesian-looking spindly construction of the long
    jetty with its crane;
the gull-molested fishing boats;
the timber boat, being slowly trodden down, before
    disappearing;
and the estuary, that often held an ochre sandbank
of perfect river-pebble shape —
looked out across the ocean, that was momentarily
    changing, and too huge to really look at, stretching
    the mind apart.
All this is gone now, of course, under concrete flats and
    shops, car-parks, and a highway;
even the sea has been largely blocked out —
we shall sleep no more.

And I am like a salmon, that can't forget the place where
    it was born
and only wants to return there. Nowhere
is like that any longer.

What I most often remember now, of all that time,
is just one afternoon. I had come home early from
    school, on my own, and my mother called me
to get the washing in.
Clouds were coming up like the Zulu tribes.
And it seemed such a big deal, to be helping your
    mother in this way, when she was excited —
she was flying along the clothes-line, plucking leaf and
    flower.
There was a train's whistle
from the shunting yard. I carried everything —
it was bundled into a sheet, and slung across my
    shoulder. The first raindrops,
blown, I told myself were spears
all around me, as I was jerked about, and bounced, run-
    ning up the backyard. Some big splattered wounds,
but I made it
onto the verandah. Getting dark in there, behind the
    trellis,
where leaves were scraping. And she spoilt it all,
by throwing inside a floorcloth, and a ragged bathmat,
    and running out into battle again
for the peg box — which I'd have done. She came back
    soaked, soaked all over,
in a suddenly steaming rain. No on could have survived
    it —
I dropped that game, not to think of such a thing.

For Harriet

A pewter-coloured,
atomized steam

is left in the early, sunlit
bathroom,

and there the child has made
a cameo

of privacy. I pass
that smoke-breathing

doorway, and see how she has stepped
down

into the fields of women;
stooped

with hair-brush
to the first harvest

of her
uncertain pleasures.

At the Inlet

1

    In the dawn an eagle leaves the forest; now the flat sea is
lichened with the sun. The fish will be sparks of darkness,
pouring through the water. And those thick-fingered long
wings cup and undulate, loose and watery on the air.

2

    Thus nature maintains itself without my concurrence;
before it all my subjectivity has no standing and is dissolved. In
taking it to myself, I find an incomparable satisfaction.

3

While the surrealists, who sought the Marvellous, that is hidden somewhere within us, have produced only the grotesque. How detestable, their facile sacrifice of the beauty which things have —

4

The dust on a sunlit window-pane; the life of the pores, of the hairs along the shin; the globed moisture on the upper lip; and the nipple, made of little packed, flattened globes, like a boysenberry, unripe pink. Inevitable that I should think of D., 'the bird of loudest lay' ...

5

I've opened the petals on the bud in her flesh. Branches ache around the powdered moon; contralto stars. She arches on her back; her face is soaring; her breasts seem wind-compacted. The lights of a town across the bay, like the broken streamers of our departure. And a salty snail-glitter of stars down the glass.

6

Is this world of ours being scattered, the flying rubble from burst Paradise? So my mother taught, but I can only believe it when overlong in the cities, amongst other men.

7

Nature, in Chinese religion, is the creator of itself. It is not necessarily benign nor hostile to man, who is just a part, and must find his place within its being. The name of this teaching is sanity.

8

A ladle has been hung by an open kitchen window. Forest, ocean, sky.

9

With the natural object, an artist has all he needs to express himself. This dictum of Pound's was foreseen by Aristotle: Nothing in the mind that isn't first in the senses. Therefore, it can be said that life's fulfilment is in the contemplation of matter.

10

The true nature of the world is not different to the things we see. 'One should not cling to an essence that is separate from the outside of things. When one sees mountains and rivers, he sees the Buddha-nature: when one sees the Buddha-nature, he sees the cheeks of a donkey or the mouth of a horse.'

11

An early morning sea with a row of streetlights burning, a bare railway platform, and the few late stars. All that has beauty in human experience only exists this way because of death.

12

And the nothingness of death is not so vast or terrible; it is more like something intimate. It's of my size, exactly.

13

Since the ego of an individual can be shown to be an illusion (which we experience as estrangement and lifelessness), any philosophy that finds an ego in the universe — God, or some abiding Absolute — reinforcing, and rising out of, such illusion, must itself be equally false.

14

The fibrous grasses that grow sparsely across the sandhills flicker. If grass were measured on a scale beside water, this would be a trickle from rusty pipes. And the broken palings of the back fence are plaited with old bloodied strands of wire. The fence sags full of sand, and yet is eloquent as a mainsail, in its curving before the sea.

Mr Nelson

Their house was old grey weatherboards, on a small
 town back-street
of shale and potholes and white dust;
the verandah in lattice
from which some last off-white paint was almost gone.
It was down a slope,
on low posts that were hidden by blue hydrangeas
at the front, and had two concrete steps, and a steep,
 gravel-rashed iron roof.
The picket fence was unpainted, also,
tall paspalum
growing amongst it, where the scythe or push-mower
 couldn't reach.
I used carefully to pull a long, pale strand
of that round grass
from deep in its coarse outer sheaths, not breaking it,
 getting a very long
curved frond, and would lightly
touch my mother's arm
with the asymmetrical head, while she was talking over
 the fence there,
to get her to come along.

Almost all of the houses on that sunlight-dragged,
 smoke-idling street
were alike, except those with louvres
above their verandah sides, or a faded canvas blind.
A few newer places, in fibro,
had flat roofs, and were painted
with army surplus undercoat, pink or aquamarine.
Where some young people lived, I remember,
there'd be an old car in the front yard, its parts
 seemingly always spread on the grass,
and a wireless playing loudly from indoors.
The songs I'd hear,
my forehead leaned against the fence, while flattening an
 ants' nest with my shoe,

or trying to heap it up again,
were things like 'Ghost Riders in the Sky', and 'The Streets of
    Laredo',
and 'Half As Much':
If you lo-ved me halfasmuch as I love you,
You wouldn't st-ay a-way halfasmuch as you do,
sung by a whiny female voice.

Along the top of the low, cleared hills, behind those deep
    backyards,
there was some remaining bush, and this
used to seem so dreary,
like the old cooking-splatters and fly-specklings of a kitchen
    wall.

Mrs Nelson would come out
to talk with my mother over the fence;
small and dried-up
with a voice like little bundles of twigs snapping and giving.
She was nervous-eyed as a hen,
and had a very hollow throat, inside its slack strings.
She'd had a young daughter, killed by a car
when riding a bike,
and so my mother used to always speak of Mrs Nelson as
    'that poor thing'.

Standing at their front gate, making the latch click open and
    shut, gently,
careful not to be told, in mid-conversation, to get away,
or to have my hand slapped,
I could look down into their door and through the house, out
    to the bright-lit,
bleached backyard, with its long sapling clothes-line poles
that held up tea-towels, sheets, and bloomers.
And I'd sometimes see Mr Nelson's shape,
his prolapsed stomach, in the blue singlet he always wore,
crossing their kitchen, at the end of the hall. Barefoot on the
    lino, he carried
a teapot and newspaper,

or half a loaf of bread on its board, or a tin of jam
with open, serrated top. Sometimes he'd come out
and offer me a Ginger Nut biscuit, if he saw me looking
    through the gate-slats,
and then he'd say, just a bit more loudly,
'Your copper's boiling.'
He seemed a peculiar man,
diffident even with a child, and so polite and embarrassed
    with my mother.
He had a broad, cracked face, with what I see now
as a glaze of grief over it,
that had seemed then like a feeling of sickness, in the
    light,
and so I suppose I'm remembering him from shortly
    after his daughter's 'accident'.

One time my mother told me, after we'd left their gate
    and were hurrying on,
going to visit my grandparents around the corner,
    something else
about the Nelsons.
— I don't know what Mr Nelson's job was, although I
    remember
he once wore black sump-oil boots,
but he evidently could walk home through the cemetery,
at the end of their street, where the daughter was buried,
and he must have got off early, as Council workers do,
    because this happened
in hot afternoon sun.
(I've seen the cemetery there at such a time:
glary marble along the hill, amongst orange clay and
    grey, poor grass,
underneath a sudden cliff-face of dark bush,
with cicadas shrilling
in the heat so loud they made your head feel
it was being spun rapidly within.)
Among those dusty, bleached-out plastic flowers, and the
    jars of black water,

145

Mr Nelson had come on a large brown snake,
curled in the sun, on a grave-top.
He'd looked for something to kill it with, creeping off
backwards, and had only been able to grab a bit of rusty
    iron fence
from a sunken grave, that he could work loose, that had
lumps of concrete sticking to it,
and he struck with this —
but the metal was awkwardly bent, he was hitting onto
the hill below, and the snake
had sensed him, so that even though he swung several times,
    it got away,
into a hole down the side of someone's grave.
The trouble was, he'd been seen
from a distance, seemingly smashing about,
by a person who had gone and told the minister, who'd
inspected, and told the police, and so on. That bit of rail
was decorated and barbed, and had scratched the headstone's
    face
as he tried to bash close beside it. Mrs Nelson said to Mum
that for the damage he'd caused
they were being sued by someone or other, a big noise
    in town.
And they had no money,
with the funeral expenses, recently. My mother was 'very sad'
    and annoyed
over this happening at such a time 'to that poor woman'.

When I was about fifteen, with a taste for Romantic poetry,
I used to wander around in the graveyard sometimes — my
    grandparents were there by then —
where I once found
a heavily scratched and chipped headstone. (Perhaps the case
    against Mr Nelson had been lost,
or the money was used for something else.) And I could work
    out,
mainly with my fingertips,
that there'd been a particularly unctuous verse, something
    about

God wanting the best early, for Himself,
once carved upon it.

'Following the wheel tracks ...'

Following the wheel tracks, that had long been overgrown,
he came at length to the end of the forest. And the whole sky,
from all the dark horizons, was adrift with grazing stars. After
a while, it seemed those stars were dangled water, and the fresh-
ness of the night was breathed from them. In the dim fields
below the hillside, nothing moved. Except, far off, among some
clumps of trees, which were merely slightly darker stains, a
light, occasionally travelling. He wasn't sure, but perhaps the
faintest sound reached him, hung in immensity, from that
distant road.

Curriculum Vitae

1

Once, playing cricket, beneath a toast-dry hill,
I heard the bat crack, but watched a moment longer
a swallow, racing lightly, just above the ground. I was
    impressed by the way
the bird skimmed, fast as a cricket ball.
It was decided for me, within that instant,
where my interests lay.

And the trajectories at dusk of random moths and
    lone decisive swallow
will often still preoccupy me, until dew occludes the air.

2

I can remember there were swallows that used to
    sew together
the bars of a cattle yard.
I would be sitting in morning sunlight

on the top rail, to feel its polished surface
beneath my hands.
A silvery, weathered log that had the sheen of thistle's flax.

3

A cow was in the stocks with the calm expression of a Quaker;
and my father stretched his fingers,
a pianist seated on a chopping block. He bent his forehead to
  an instrument
out of Heath Robinson —
a dangling bagpipes, big as a piano,
that was played by tugging on organ stops.
The cow began to loosen its milk: its teats were disgorged,
the size and colour of small carrots;
and milk was flourished in the bucket, two skewer-thin daggers
sharpened on each other underhand.
Then, as the bucket filled, there would be the sound of a
  tap running
into deep suds at the end of a bath.
Finally, the calf was let in,
and this sounded like a workman building-up a big lather
  between his hands.

The concrete in those bails was shattered, but lay together
as though a platform of river stones; and water ran there
  constantly
from a hose, breaking up and bearing off
the hot lava of any cow-pats. That water was delicate and
  closely-branched —
a long weed fluttering, on such a breezy morning.

4

There were great dents of cloud-shadow on the blue-
  forested mountain;
and far off, over
the paddocks, through midday heat, the fluttering silk scarf
of a light purple range.
Our mountain was the kite, and those in the distance, its tail,
through all the heat-wavering days.

And many broken, dead trees had been left standing
    about,
like stone ruins: pillars that held out the remnants
of cloisters and fine stonework,
with rubble beneath them. But the air was so clear;
    so uncrowded
with any past —
arbitrary corridors, unpeopled, through the air.
Room for the mind to travel on and on.
I used to have to stop, often, to stand there, in that
    immense amphitheatre
of silence and light.

5

I remember watching our three or four geese let loose
    and rushing,
with their heads beating sideways like metronomes,
towards a dam where the mountain-top hung;
and when they entered the water, the mountain's image
    came apart
suddenly, the way a cabbage falls into coleslaw.
Everything was changed, as easily as that.

6

Since then, I have been, for instance, in Petticoat Lane —
    pushing by
through narrow, stacked alleys,
among the tons of rotting garbage for sale,
and have seen the really poor.
Those people seemed just dangling paper dolls, threaded
    onto
a genetic string —
the characters of poverty, starch, lack of sun,
and stunted, hopeless spirit everywhere. Their crossed
    eyes, warts,
twisted faces, snaggle teeth,
drunkenness were Dickens still, in '70 something,

again in '82. — People in greasy rags, on crutches, weeding
    wet butts
from the gutters;
spiky-haired, furtive, foul-muttering.
The women were shaped like slapped-together piles of clay.
    They scrabbled
amongst junk, viciously,
yelling to each other, and oblivious. . . .

What is such an evil, but the continuing effect
of capital's Stalinism?
Enclosure, as John Clare has said, lets not a thing remain.

And then, an hour later, in the West End I found
how much worse I thought an askance,
meringue-coloured, prissy-lipped upperclass face — so sleek
in its obliviousness.
People go rotten with culture, also.

7

Another time, in Washington, when my girlfriend had gone
to see someone,
and while I was sitting at an upstairs window, I watched the
    bald man
who lived next door, after he'd argued once more
with his wife, come out to stand alone
in their backyard — round as a pebble, in his singlet,
but nowhere near so hard.
He was standing with chin sunk,
holding the garden hose — a narrowed stream
he felt around with
closely, like a blind man's cane.
It disturbed me to see him like that — and then, as I
    started to consider myself,
I saw that I was walking
in those silver paddocks, again,
which as a kid I'd known.

8

Or travelling alone in Europe once, and staying in a
    provincial city,
indolent and homesick of an afternoon,
I turned, as ever, to the museum.
In such a mood, however, the masterpiece will often no
    longer serve:
it seems too strenuous and too elevated;
it belongs in a world too far beyond one's own.
From experience, one has learned at these times to follow
    that arrow, *École française*
XIXe siècle. There, on an attic floor,
unnoticed by the attendant, a newspaper crumpled
over his boots, or along the deserted outer corridors,
beneath tall windows, in the light from which
many of them are cancelled,
hang one's faithful mediocrities — in sympathy with whom
one had thought to be borne through until dinnertime.
Armand Guillaumin, Léon Cogniet, Jules Dupré, Félix Ziem:
no artistic claims can be made for these. Their sluggish or
    bituminous pigment,
greasy sheen, and craquelure,
their failures, so complex and sad, have earned them
'an undisturbed repose'.
And yet, even these harmless,
unassuming, and forgotten, as I glanced among them, on
    this occasion,
were forgotten
by their one idle, arbitrary re-creator,
and the landscapes that came far more vividly before my eyes
were all memories.

9

Into my mind there has always come, when travelling,
images of the twisted Hawkesbury bush
crackling in the heat, and scattering its bark and twigs
    about,

white sunlight flicked
thickly on the frothy surges
and troughs of its greenery; and within those forests,
great pools of deep fern, afloat
beneath a sandstone rock-lip; and of the Platonic blueness
of the sky; and recollections of Coledale and Thirroul
on their clifftops, where sea-spray
blows among the pines and eucalypts; and, most of all, of
    those forests,
cool, light-flouncing, with white female limbs,
and the yeasted green pastures,
where my mind first opened, like a bubble from a
    glass-blower's tube,
and shone, reflecting
things as they are —
there, where I have felt, anxiously, I would find them
a while longer,
after passing Kempsey, once more, on the mail train of an
    early morning.

Piano

Black Landscape

All of the high country, that year, had been burned out
with the headline blackness of war.
Soon afterwards we came travelling through the place,
along a ridge's blade-edge by car.

The tree-forms then were the crudest of hieroglyphs —
a crushed charcoal scrawl;
petrified in their extreme gestures, about those hills
steep as a landslide sprawl.

Rain-storms had just been there; in overcast light
boulders exuding shine.
And the clinkered valleys were backed with high, wet cliffs.
An immense open-cut coal mine.

We were creeping through winds that pounded on the car;
twanged it; made it a cripple;
that seemed to compress its shape. But stopped to photograph;
the car braced like a mule.

Climbed down, into stillness and deadness. The clay slopes'
squirming runnels, closely traced,
left earth hung between horizontal strata — a Hindu facade,
now almost effaced.

A crow was blown away, with a shout; I thought of having to eat
such dry fibre. Keats didn't know
all about those syllables, 'forlorn', who'd never heard
a sound like the bushfire's crow.

Everywhere, great ruptured webs, the shining charcoal bushes.
Twigs traced and smudged us black.
I saw ahead, in profile, how a cliff-face was built of shale:
the silverfishes' newspaper stack.

Smell of wet ashes, and trickling of water. We found
headless trees breaking there
into fine leaves, again: the boles were stockinged with them
as with flame. A tremulous mohair.

In red and green of an apple. So: fire, air, water, earth;
each contending with another;
shifting of energies, as animals shove in their sleep. And life,
too, where things are sore.

I took from beneath a stone the cicada: six-legged tottering;
three clear jewels on its brow;
a samurai's orange mask. Those beautiful gauze wings
segmented with a gum tree bough.

Between such branches, if you tilt your hand, you can make
a light, pale blue and frail
as after sunset. I told a girl once, in Ireland, of cicadas;
she said, 'We only ever had a snail.'

Configuration

Smoke is stirring its haunches slowly
at the dark end of the platform —
the nebulae.

The tall heads of weeds are frail
in a sparse lamp-light
over gravel.

In the waiting room, a viscous shine
on plank walls and benches,
sluggish green.

We are waiting outside, at the edge
of the varnished light;
our breaths merge.

Space and night, and the windy rush
of the train, far off
in the bush.

The stars are a salt-freighted wind
where the Department's red lights
are pinned.

Matins

The bricks drawn off the brick stack,
two together, scrape on their brick dust
and clink and chime, glassily and brittle,
as they're stacked afresh, into his barrow
by the bricklayer's mate, who wears
large gloves, that are mauve and stiff as
old rabbit hides. The bricklayer's mud
lies stirred and ready on its boards,
with the same colour, and looseness,
and pendulous weight, as an elephant's
haunch. The off-sider's boots scuff
the smears of mortar across the pavement,
grind on pebbles, resound hollowly in the
slack board ramp, on which they tramp,
making a single loose bass string's sound —
desultorily and thickly-fingered struck.
Orange-red leaves will be dripping from
the pavement trees, under a grey sky,
about the kerb: whimsical and idle like
an Ophelia's petals, and yet serious, too.
The trees' sift is counterpoint to all that
stomping, or the shearing, gravel-slicing
sound of the spatula, that knocks and
is drawn again, through its grating slide.
All the time, sparrows hop like hot fat,
underneath a dim tree, making their sharp
decibels of sound, over and over, or stop
to puff and rewind the simple mechanism

of excess. And now, a long underbelly sound
of a tarpaulin, dragged upon to slide.
And I hear the steady, firm high heels of
what must be a young woman passing by,
and this knocking is not hollow, the way
workmen's noise is, nor like the traffic,
harried, and how it builds a calf and thigh,
and buttocks, and those rower's cables,
the spinal muscles, that are shaped by light,
and sheened, and finally has called me up
out of the deep blankets, to the day.

A Port of Europe

Like a bandage in a gorse bush, water gleams
on the dark-clouded moor,
and far off, in the other direction, along the top of
      the world,
lies a slat of metal ocean, under
brittle moonlight.
The moon is resonant on the sea, as though a
      gong-face were flicked
with a fingernail.
And one dark, cowled farmhouse, with chalky jowls,
      drowses
stiffly here, in a hallway for the winds —
it is the nun who keeps a door.
Westward from Flensburg, on these low marshlands
of saturated green,
air capers wildly
as children of the poltergeist,
vaulting far over the metronome monotony of
      windmills, and the few small startled horses
with wind-hacked manes.
The shoreline and fields are mere sediment of a
      coagulating sky.
The ocean shifts as though weight-lifted oil,
and under old jetties undulates

lubriciously as crazed inmates on the poles.
Black outer waters of ocean jostle
and bound, a herd of migrant tusks, that mills and
    advances again,
and fills one with dread, imagining
the blankly inhuman nature
of a primal force.
A small town flies the moon with its flags,
among casques of verdigris. The landscape stares in,
    down the streets,
and carries within its cloak
the cock of mockery.
Spires and clock-chimes, and beneath them a few sails
cupped and pulsing softly, like pale jelly-fish;
and long water-logged barges
that burrow in a deep grey or moss-black estuarine water.
Over the acres of sea-front, dieseline
and urinous salt. Here, the parlours of casseroles and
    geraniums,
of alcohol, onion-rings, pipe smoke,
and old fish-nets dried as roots. A patina of human
    grease
is on every stone and sill. And these scratched, pewter-
    coloured faces —
are these the heads of tragic clowns,
or snouts, in trampled water?
The clouds at sunset were vast, lurid fungi:
damp purples, yellows, and vermilion. One sail
like a drifting spore —
the long-tailed seed of a pine cone, that had burst in a
    distant fire —
was wavering there,
towards what seemed the mountainous country of the sky;
but it will have fallen again
upon this shore.

Very Early

Birds are drifting, bubbles on the eyesight, in a frangipani
    sunrise.
Waves nod as a rocking horse would,
if it were one that left standing before long windows could
stir with the air. Now on the bay lies
the diamond flotilla. And right the length of the harbour
a light stretches: one duellist, and the other.

The weavings of an immediate Penelope; and then, a vast
    trunk of light
speckled about with a leaf-shimmer
of light-points. On many a verandah
you see where the summer mist of the mosquito net
is still abroad. The hypotenuse at ease.
Curlicues on a dog's back are being planed by a breeze.

The dog, tongue loose as a pocket hanging out,
is leaving the reserve (these roman candles of green,
the lawns pebbly with dew, and moored yachts with their
    bathroom sheen);
it blows away into the open barn door of a street —
dimly and complacent, follows some hunch.
A small, dark bird in there shifts like a sparkle on a
    branch.

Here at the park, a turbaned snail, the potentate of the dew,
majestically moves. Gum leaves are eyebrows being drawn
on light. A spider hangs in the midst of dawn.
The pine trees, at a distance, seem water-stains down a
    plastery blue.
If no-one saw all this, its existence would go on just as well.
And what is really here no words can tell.

Rainy Windows

Wildly flourished, little pods of water;
and these long runnels, drawn among them, for the stalks —
it is a frieze of shivery grass.

A puffed diffidence, of floaty, pattered weeds.
Or a carbonated glass, in which the apothegmatic bubbles
are pressured down.

Through gauzy water, gate-posts,
tiles, chimneys, black tentacles, and the sudden leaf-twitches
of birds leaping, without birds.

The pavement twitches. Out there,
the land of 'the Anthropophagi, and (of those) whose heads
    do grow
beneath their shoulders.'

Across my room, a window's lizard skin,
silverish-grey. Going over, the world is in all the jumbled
colours, and fogginess, of a wok.

One keeps returning: to what's also the smudge
on chilled white grapes. Within it, the light of a
    chardonnay.
Approached, a fluttery veil — frail

and dotty. A Zelda Fitzgerald, though one
calmer now. This tender collector of sodden lengths
    of string.
Along the road, soda fuzziness

as lights appear in late afternoon.
It has all become a watercolourist's first essay, washed off
beneath the tap. A miscegenated grey.

In such weather, only largeness matters,
bases endure. The watcher's allowed an intimation of
    release
in the detachment of this flickery change.

I always find with such weather an utter
accord. As when, grown still, one lies sidelong to consider
the perspiring face of one's love.

Byron Bay: Winter

Barely contained by the eyesight,
the beach makes one great arc —
blue ranges, overlapped behind it;
each of them is a tide-mark.

About me, swamp-oaks' foliage
streams: hatching by Cézanne.
Out on the heath, a guard's carriage
follows the vats of a train.

A creek spoils the hem of the sea,
spread on the beach in flutes:
it's from a swamp, red as black tea,
that smelt of sodden roots.

Behind, cloudy afternoon swells,
the colour of claret stain.
Sunlit town, or midden of shells.
The lighthouse, a tiny pawn.

I'm walking on the beach alone;
the sea's grey feathers flurry,
showing emerald. Sandpipers blown
seem mice, in their scurry.

And the sun on my shoulders brings,
because of its perfect warmth,
the feeling that I wear great wings
while stepping along the earth.

A Garden Shed

From ten to thirteen I was often sent
for a month or even more at a time
to my grandmother's in a distant town
after grandfather died — it was thought
I should go, though she hardly spoke.

I read by the stove; she would pause
in sewing, sometimes, and you'd see
she was out billowing about, or
crouching beside doors along the night,
pushing at some. I kept a watch;

but after school I used to wander
in the scrub behind that big-verandahed,
shabby, dislocated bungalow, beyond
her call and the other straggling houses
at the town's edge; and I saw how

once in the country the train began
wildly careering, with its horn
braying out, again and again.
When I arrived first, rain appeared:
long slashes on a carriage window

that broke up those trajectories,
so the heavy glass it seemed was chipped
at, but slowly — too slowly for escape.
I remember the clattering of a tocsin,
the railway crossing that we burst

right through — a clown and hoop;
and I was driven on, landed, lips stretched,
on my feet. It must have been
the ache at her house was the boredom,
since it was never really so good

being at home. But the mountains between,
above small-town, dairy farm smoke,
were a kingfisher blue, and their glint,
coming from night, was sad like a sail
that passes by. Strange you don't complain

at that age. I had the inarticulate
endurance children have, or some have.
Grandma died of her strokes, completely mad.
I'd only liked there when allowed a key
to grandfather's shed. 'Just so's to look.'

At the end of the long, rubbishy yard,
past lumber on trestles, the chicken run
of oil-black earth and wire netting,
the tatty eucalypts with their clothes line,
all in a high stockade of palings,

I let myself in. There, I'd rediscover
each chisel, peculiar saws, the claw
and ballpein hammers, his screwdrivers,
brace-and-bits, punches, spanners, and
a regal, African paint brush array,

stood on shakily-done shadowboards —
things spiky, knobbed, sharp or frayed
like those raced among, beyond the fence,
out in the heath. I'd handle these,
but it would have been sacrilege for me

to think them useable. (It was there
I was betrayed, my family would say.)
All of that was carefully hung,
sharp and oiled, in the gloom again,
with glints — strange, like creatures in

(were it possible) a deep-sea aquarium.
And I found beneath the workbench
sawdust still adrift in a spider's web.
There was an old sofa, brown, bleached
as though a rose petal in a book;

and stacks of bevelled, collected timber
slung overhead — how curious those
differing lengths: each had a meaning,
I felt, like poetry-shapes to be read
some day in our maroon leather Milton.

Grimy light in there made it look
always a rainy afternoon. In the quiet
I could hear the neighbour's hens creak
just outside, or washing flap,
or a car somewhere, changing gear.

And I've always wanted to live again
at the level where one lived when
looking at, or listening to, those things:
in the immense presence of that wordless
questioning. I seemed to be lying alone

out on a hillslope, until I could hear
coming through things cast-up about there
a far roaring, of their endless sea.
In the secret noise of such turmoil
and spray, I was somehow looking back —

or being looked through, about to be lost —
to my grandfather and I, who were only

bubbles of a moment, amid this whirling
away. I first recognized the frankness
of nature's appropriations there:

that it's all effectiveness, inter-response;
all mutuality and possibilities;
just things happening among themselves.
Things creating each other. And we
are only the expressions of circumstance,

of its tensions. Nothing belongs to any
separate thing. It was there I began
to understand: the less we think we are
the more we bear; and someone who sees
he is nothing, lightly will bear it all.

Harbour Dusk

She and I came wandering there through an empty park,
and we laid our hands on a stone parapet's
fading life. Before us, across the oily, aubergine dark
of the harbour, we could make out yachts —

beneath an overcast sky, that was mauve underlit,
against a far shore of dark, crumbling bush.
Part of the city, to our left, was fruit shop bright.
After the summer day, a huge, moist hush.

The yachts were far across their empty fields of water.
One, at times, was gently rested like a quill.
They seemed to whisper, slipping amongst each other,
always hovering, as though resolve were ill.

Away off, through the strung Bridge, a sky of mulberry
and orange chiffon. Mauve-grey, each cloven sail —
like nursing sisters, in a deep corridor: some melancholy;
or nuns, going to an evening confessional.

Eight Poems after Kusadao

two
things

that have
no

memories

fresh

fallen
snow

a

leaping

squirrel

—

at
dawn

three or
four

often

to say
they're

wronged

—

cutting
at

the
cabbage

heart

and
a rooster

calls
far

off

in
huge

desolation

—

my
wife

two
nights

gone
for

two
nights

the
galaxy

—

a
plum

bloom
trodden

down
shows

us
this

earth

—

late
night

apples
lamp-

lit
stall

and
Orion

in glory

—

zazen
in

temple
cold

so
harsh
my

eyes
trickle

hopeless

longing

—

autumn

I
hear

cicadas
grow

fainter

with
no

resistance

Nakamura Kusadao, haiku poet, 1901-1984.
Translated with Professor Shigeo Kitagawa, Tokyo, 1985.

Plurality

To Philip Hammial, the traveller from an antique land

Our flat was in a building which backed onto the golf course,
and it shone with the bay. In this street,
hosannas of Mediterranean palms, and Moreton Bay fig trees
pressing large fingers to the light.
Here we lived day after day.

A concrete esplanade, planted with old metal lamp-posts,
shaped the waterfront. The bay's wobble
when the tide was running in
was like the filled reboundings of a spirit level.
Or the water grey and heavy as a punt.

This also had its beauty. If a tug or trawler came
from under leaves, on such a day,
the bow-wave was luminously white. And gangly yachts,
subtly restless, as though they were a schoolgirls' assembly,
waited — their gowns, umbrellas rolled tight.

Out in the harbour, along the moored steamers' high
    black sides,
drifting up and down, dropping like shuttles
down a spindle, levered up again — for their tensile
wide-orbiting dance — were gulls.
The dreaming efficiency of machine parts, in the distance.

From our windows late, with lights out, the water shimmering
as if leaves on a tree,
the way it was lifted in the moonlight. And further on, toward
the moon, the harbour so gauze-like it could be
a desert — untrodden, silvery-dewed.

This was, for me, the tranquil early eighties; I was not yet forty.
I've mostly lived near the sea;
part of my boyhood was remote, in the face of empty water.
I think at the end we live a similar way.
In those days, it was on a headland, yellow and dusty.

The tall sea could seem, at once, a wall and its isolate
forbidden garden. (O fertile, impossible sea.)
The earth there, with a scumbling of tight grass, was in
     the summer
zwieback. A few weatherboard houses, dry
as folds of a lizard's throat, before the jangled light.

Washing waved to nothing. Our side wall transformed
in late afternoon, like a filled sponge. For play, as a kid,
I'd a myriad small antheaps — their energy of boiling
     saucepans.
The clouds often like a motorcycle skid.
Beyond the stale mustard-colour of land, a ship went
     traipsing.

Quartz gravel, dandelions, rusty tin, the blown
dirt road, slant telephone poles, a reservoir. . . .
Then, below our flat, someone swaying on a moisturized
     golf-course
beside the bay, posed like a figurine for us to admire.
I don't forget the real nature of the ocean.

If you live with that, and little else, it will come to seem
     a dream
that is fed with dreams. It deals, then keeps on and on
to regain. It's both good and evil
and will not resolve itself where you draw a line.
Long fumbling to describe it, I heard of the sky
     burial.

In Tibet, when someone ordinary dies, because the earth
     is sacred,
and there's such scarcity of wood,
they're laid on a large rock outside town, where an
     undertaker,
with two knives, goes to work — the body is dissected;
the skin flayed, all joints severed.

Male relatives watch from a short distance those gesturing
    tools
of a little squatting monkey, whom no-one
but outcasts will speak to, whom no doctor will treat,
his white robes growing silently spoiled. He has slit the body
    open
and piles the organs like jewels.

Briskly scores and dices flesh; takes a small sledge-hammer
to the bones, pounding each one;
he makes of the whole body, within three-quarters of an hour,
a neat wet pile. No pictures of this can be taken.
Into bones and flesh stirs some barley-meal.

Finally stands back, and holding wide his hands, stiff as
    prods,
those two weird flowers, he sings,
ululates, to the eroded escarpments around, the one
    extraordinary
word, of Tibetan knife-carved lettering, that brings
thumping about him an avalanche of big, loose clods —

The vultures amble over each other's backs, and slap
monstrous gloves. Saved for the leader of the flock,
now thrown him, the liver. Trampling of waves. And those
    great wings
glisten and stream. In minutes, not a sliver on the rock.
Their flight: graceful and horrible. It cancels out.

There is nowhere valuation. Everything, equally, is desire
    to live.
It is a oneness, always plural.
Yet, if someone crosses the stale ditch about themselves,
or the yachts on blueness incarnate a breeze, or a face is
    beautiful,
how this ocean's endless hunger can seem worthwhile.

Cows in Massachusetts

The cows have left the barns, and wearing their leaf-shadow
they're all through an early spring's

treeless yet filtered air;
and they moo as they barely move about, with horns low

in the grass, that is silvery and lacquered
and has its tips curled downward, too.

Across the grass comes a breeze, and so these Friesians
seem to stand amid a pebbly ford;

grass so moist it smarts the air
when tugged upon, like fingers drawn down shiny glass.

The air in spring here is yellow
as cider, or cider apples — that crabbed fruit

propped on wet sticks; and one thinks of the yellow
of damp straw in barns,

like a hairdresser's combed snippings
amongst the dung;

and of the mellow colour of a turtle's stone
breast, tapped upon; the horn of a farmer's thumb

and dry palm; the scraped-out cold chicken fat;
grass ribbons in a book;

and in these woods, puffed onto mud, the curry powder
of a scuffed fungus

among the staircase roots. . . . But this was about the
    illusion
of God's own country seeming to be,

for a passing
few minutes, where they have claimed. And about

Jasper Johns, whom someone said that one could meet
in New York,

or Andy Warhol — 'I can fix it for you.'
But I left there

and went on, and saw the cows pass,
who know what they like, and did not think Alas.

Walking Around at Night

The rising moon appears,
softly focused as a movie queen,
in a close frame
through the kitchen fly-screen.

I stroll outside, and down the path,
leaving the radio;
the moon is buxom
above the smokily-draped willow.

It's soon the old fumy paraffin lamp
of a moon, that I prefer.
The hammer blows of barking,
a car clearing its chest, somewhere,

the slam of a tinny garage door
on concrete, and the voices
going inside, that could be either quarrelsome
or boisterous.

A torn white paper edging
of water in a gutter.
The poplars and bushes, that are waiting for me to pass,
are dressed in *purdah*.

This dim-lit town backs
into black gullies, from the milkbar freeway:
a few novas burn
in a shapeless, dusty galaxy.

Cars and pick-up trucks pulled on the grass
under porch-shine
have a cold, metallic baldness
where the dew is strewn.

The white-painted boards of one house
wear a net veil
of leaf-shadows. These lawns, side-lit,
are wheatgrass; succulent, shapely, and frail.

The parking lot is bare tonight
within a cold, immense
chain-wire, on which I hang. The shadows of some
    pebbles
loom like a chess defence.

A single tree on the lawn beside here,
in 'subdued light', is still:
dressed up like a woman, alone in the corridor
of a convention hotel;

a skinny tree, in knee-length fashion, and
leg-aligning, high-heel pose.
Now, a little nervous, and preening — already tottery.
Another one of those.

This way, just out of town, is a tall hill-shape —
a dark, perfect dune —
unravelling irregularly as coarse cloth
its outline, under the moon.

A set of headlights is coming beneath it,
here, in colder air
from the river. I turn into the paddocks,
toward a steamy, lit fun-fair,

that's been isolated by the wind tonight
at the racecourse. I only go so near.
The music, heavy-handed makeup,
and those lights are overflowing like beer.

The rides: slow poker machines, or big-jointed lumberings.
Glazed with luminous breath,
there's a long headland of forest behind
the sad necklace of milk teeth.

Across the paddocks, backyards —
above the fences, lounge room lights burn;
in the frosty night, thick like thistle fur,
a few porch lights are on.

I keep walking, and see that a cow and the moon
are each a term
in some kind of sequence. I shoo
a cow up, for a place to lie that's warm,

under a lichen-smoke and bird's egg sky.
Adrift on the windmill night.
It gets chill. Going on, toward a razor-strop highway —
that sound, those streaks of light.

They are suddenly lifted away at the curve
and gone — each a stroke;
and there's an occasional heavy flat backward
stropping, which is a truck.

Waiting to cross (a short-cut back), I stand off
in the weeds. At every car,
these are strung with glutinous, distended drops.
The moon's blue as an old scar.

Prunus Nigra

The plum tree with popcorn blossom
is pink upon the frost,
or it's embossed on the dusty blueness
of the lower sky, toward dusk.

A magpie, ragged witch-doctor,
long-jumps to the clothes-line pole;
behind it, the plum tree bursts
like a wave at sunset.

How terrible it would be
if this plum bloomed near the palings
and one saw it with the memories
of some other life.

Fire Sermon

The lissome bay is silvered slightly, in its supine lightness;
a stocking-textured water
takes the morning's cerise.

But soon, between the headlands, sea and sky are solid blues
that have closed, almost
seamlessly, like stone.

And yachts have come out to climb on the sea's face, slow
and wavering — the way
that cabbagemoths walk.

These foreshores are deeply tented in eucalyptus saplings
and tea-trees, leaned
on the engorged light.

Here cicadas' sizzling, strapped toffee strings of sound,
filmy and flashing, fuse
into sheets, all around.

Now the rhythmical light-points shoal the water thickly
as this shift to shovelled
gravel in cicadas' song.

Simmered eucalyptus oil vaporously uncoils, accompanying
angophoras, the dancing
Indras of rosy stone.

Dilated summer. It seems you can see into the Flame, while
light-cells teem, cicadas thrum —
to its naked sensuous events.

On the far shore, house-faces hang, a white muslin among
bush humble as rubble
in the blue Empire.

I've left everything behind, for an endpaper shore; to lie
under membranous layers, as
lights vault, coagulate, rebound —

To see one ignite another, billowing, and genealogies decline;
to watch here day's ardour
that turns water into wine.

Other People

There are rain-pebbles, late,
across black windows, streetlight on them;
they hang like conglomerate
in the cement wall of a mausoleum,

which is the darkness. Or are fused
as if a lever were thrown
when cars pass. Clear dark is bruised
where a figure sits. The telephone

keeps on. Headlights splash as though
trying to wash from the wall
a realization. One that won't let go
for anyone who'd call.

—

A public phone and pine trees on
the edge of the paddocks. You see a man
crossing an oily concrete apron
to the shop's bowser. An old beer can

in here, a cigarette's long ash
on the ledge. The directory says, 'My Fault',
underscored. 'Come on Babe.' Your cash
dangles. Echo-sounds a black vault.

The cow's rump is a rowboat that takes
a wave-crest. Gritty miniatures.
A camphor laurel's lime and silver flakes.
A cloud like steam, claws over claws.

16 Poems from the Japanese

Even now, I never linger
by this valley stream,
in case my shadow
flows back into the world.
— Dōgen

Ah, how many dewdrops are falling
from the stems of grass,
now that the autumn winds have come
to the fields of Miyagino?
— Saigyo

Sorcerer, who flies through heaven,
find for me the one
who has never yet appeared,
not even in my dreams.
— Murasaki

In the shade of a willow
by the road
the clear water is running.
I meant to pause here
only a moment.
— Saigyo

Water drips from moss
among the mountain stones,
and I am rendered clear.
— Ryokan

The days that have gone by
leave one sad,
and yet they were all of them
only a dream.
— Former Emperor Hanazono

I sit and look back on
days that have gone.
Did I dream them all,
am I dreaming now?
Listening to winter rain.
— Ryokan

A light snowfall
and within that
a billion worlds arise
and within that
a light snowfall.
— Ryokan

Haze rises
at the end of a spring day
that I have spent with children
bouncing ball.
— Ryokan

As the sunset ends
and the mountains are hidden,
further off
other mountains appear.
— Kyoguku Tamekame

In my home town
the cherries are in bloom
and spring is passing by
the same as ever.
— Dōgen

Early summer rain
has left in the roadway
a hall of light.
                    — Basho

Ah, look!
The mushroom-gatherers missed
five dewdrops.
                    — Buson

A camellia fell;
the monk smiled
going by.
                    — Hori Bakusui

Clear autumn day;
my wife doesn't even notice
we pass each other.
                    — Nishigaki Shu

The crows' calling
ends.
Twilight snow.
                    —Aro Usuda

Translated with Kazuaki Tanahashi; Zen Centre, San Francisco, 1982

The Shark

There are tons of the sea's loose flesh above, made to jostle
and shimmy,
an immense, shadow-tainted
clear jelly.

It shoulders and displaces itself
about itself, on the peaked and flaked plain,
harried like migrant reindeer,
lava-bright or wind torn.

The diver goes on steadily sinking from there, spread
    on shadow
as to drown;
weighted, he feels ducked and
pole-pressured down;

only his breath seems to panic, and he turns to watch
    it pass,
wobbling and clinking upwards
into light:
a stairwell the mind climbs and breaks like glass.

The long sunlight sways here
in columns, as though a bundle of lift cables.
With its withered Red Indian head
a turtle's

struggling up steeply
on stumpy wings — an ennui, bound in horn,
a broken beak.
Bevies of fish are making little mouths to squeak

like society girls, in their spotted or banded
wafting chiffon,
and with impenetrable dead eyes. The jelly fish,
a huge heap of frog spawn.

Something stares sideways,
that has a worn-down Caligula profile — its teeth like
    a fender.
And as a spinning hoop
when it is coming to rest surrounds a

centre, with touches of all parts of the rim,
so in leathern skirt a rat-tailed
manta ray, flapping,
is hung in the grit it's flailed.

The shark comes drifting with silent engine
through water thick as smoke,
a space craft that is called on by a distant gravity
out of the murk;

but it can loosely swathe
its limber grey fuselage.
It moves with all the potential and ease of someone
turning out of a garage.

The long body wavers beautifully
and easily,
as a train at dusk
through the curves on the floor of a valley.

The gills, for all their frightful deepness,
are each neat
as a Japanese slit;
the head's simply rounded-off and incorporate

like the nose of a surfboard — it is not the authority
for anything within;
the head, amid jungle light, seems less important
than its fin.

It has the senile, yellow, ill-wishing look
of a hillbilly grandma's
uncomprehending eyes, and what seems her mouth
in its Greek mask melancholy or tooth-stump
    uncouth —

But a foolish guffaw,
and that vacuousness is filled with doubled barbed wire
or, closer,
a wreath, with each leaf a razor.

The mouth is a picketing of backward serrations;
the skin, sliding ground glass.

The diver waits with his single fang poised, for the tonnage
of its flick-pass —

imagining the voluptuous greedy wriggle
of its packed dog's body
and himself clamped too overwhelmingly, too rigid,
for struggle.

This energy, this pure appetite, that's below
and before the mind, this
is the thriving pathology
which is life; here elegant, as though wriggled from a thesis.

Weakened and divided in us, this still has to be allowed
    for,
it is basic;
in me it has a voice,
each has a shark.

And what shall we do with this?
All things are unstable and flowing, as if the modes of one
    thing:
is it possible this could modify?
It would have to be shaped through knowing.

Only through understanding,
by staying watchful and still.
The effort to change is, as with art, love, religion, a
    deviousness
of the shark-like will.

Morality we learned,
from being outdone in immorality. Ultimately, from
    Zeus.
By wanting some time
for something other than ourself. Morality is a truce.

It arises from whence
so much evil sets forth — out of boredom. But is knowledge
and strength. It's to face our nature, without wanting to
    disclaim;
to call that by its name.

Description of a Walk

In the shape of long sand-dunes, but apple green,
the pastures that I'd crossed. A quivering rain
hung above them. One currawong somewhere, warbling
happily as a hose within a drain.

The forest was cumulus on stilts, from afar;
everywhere within it, leaf-splatterings and spar;
the leaves, paint clots, or a fringe of trickling.
Angry as a burned insect, a distant car.

The forest closed. I climbed amongst sandstone —
great gouts of lava, petrified as iron;
puffed like fungi, or with a broken iceberg's edge;
all of a rusty red or burnt orange tone.

About the plinths and mantels was an artful
pebble-scatter; on its pedestal, an eccentric bowl.
Rose-coloured sandstone syncopated salt.
Blowing rain was being emptied by the bushel.

Uphill, warped arcades of bush, rack on rack;
reiterative as cuneiforms. Bacon redness of bark,
or smooth wet trunks of caterpillar green,
and some with a close dog's fur, greyish black.

Other colours: Brazil nut kernel, an unfired pot.
In the wet, tart as bush smoke, a sweet rot.
The air rain-threaded, as though with insect sounds.
My heart flapped like a lizard's, by the top.

Underneath a clay bank, an old grey gutter,
now filled — rare smoked glass. A claw of water
flexed nearby, on rock ledges, and over roots —
its wide-toothed, vibrating cane-rake clatter.

Sprigged trees, and vista of Pre-Raphaelite shine:
beneath gentian hills, a billiard table green;
ploughed land, pumpernickel; the road, a fracture;
the shapes of coral in a dark tree-line.

Rain shaded to silence. To cicadas' shekel
sound. — Emptied from a bucket, a pile of shell
poured with the numerous headlong pour of sand
onto other shells. A dry calcite rattle.

And this merely the start — warming of an engine.
Each opens a row of gills; if you find one
you see almost through the body. Their joined hums'
tremendous power, an electricity substation.

I walked on and on, in such vibrance. Wet light
gave the leaves' undersides a stainless glint.
Rag and bone bushland. White arms lifted, dangling
cloth. That chant. What it was all for I forgot.

A Winter Morning

For a few more minutes now, all the day's furniture
will remain sheeted in a shuttered room.
With their glow of sucked-thin barley sugar
the lights way off at the by-pass still drooping in
        bloom.
Here, there are only two headlights, on a lane,
easing downstairs. In wood and fibro, my cathedral
        town —
such this valley. *Materia* is *mater*; substance is womb.

I go along backyard fences through some fog —
most of these are patched with old corrugated iron —
onto a plumed, translating hillslope, with someone's dog;
high up, the sky is lifting, become woodgrain:
its whirls, dabs, darts, long streaks of golden cloud,
on airiest blue. The weeds' strung fruits wear a globed
insect's opal glitter. I skirt the dank tree-line. . . .

Those eucalyptus are the blue of husky voices.
Their elevations, declivities have all of them accents
flying. I'm here on a Sunday alone, for the offices
of matter — poinsettias, more red than sacraments;
sceptred palm-tree's golden smoulder; this insouciance
of levitated pink; grass's lime effulgence. . . .
It is the same lesson: ease of their relinquishments.

The Lake

open
screendoor

seashells

wireless
murmur

bathroom
water

louvres

ballooning
light

Small Town

Lime-green, all the lowbeamed
headlights coming by on
smoky orange dusk;
in holiday file they cross
white neon of a service station.

Much later, she again looks out,
when the highway is
a smear of grease,
and the Milky Way's blowing there,
a feather in space.

Mist

The tall trees are making a dark ravine
about this long reach of the creek
that is dark and heavy as a marble slab.
It's just before daybreak.

On the water's surface, as though teased
or kinked, there stand
fibrils of mist, balancing. Underwater,
that way, a spineless plant

lies upward. These mist-weeds
are the little splashes made by shredding
cotton wool, for a diorama.
Their suspension's really a wallowing

in slowness. It occurs on the paddocks,
too, where a single rag
is reared, eerily as the Horse-Head
Nebula, over the other fog.

Something mesmerized, sipped by the air.
Clumpy or steepled as African huts,

tree-forms are awash in the milky smoke
from a witch-doctor's rites.

Fog lingers, like white pullet feathers,
or fibres of feathers, on a woman's
busily-plucking hands. Hands ruddy and white
and thick-wristed. — The sun's

going to baste and make succulent
this earth. Even though fed with gags,
the truth will speak — will dissolve them.
Even if dead, a wet sheet that is sagged

across the empty hole of its mouth
will steam, will flutter. Or the hero's skin,
red and flawless, come forth
to accuse, as the bandages are undone.

History's a story of loss and betrayal,
and yet we're led by the earth to persevere.
Light analyses the lubricants in dew.
Only a traffic haze left in the air.

A Summer Evening

They still do as always used to be done:
they call the children just on night
then make sure of the fly-screen catch,
while moths knock down a shaggy pinch
from off themselves or the porch light.

And insects race their bobbins, thick
as a sweat shop, or a grass itch,
as matted grass seeds that get stuck
smudgily in the bleached leg-hairs.
Another sound: a nutmeg-grater scratch.

It is now the time of 'Look at yourselves!'
One not a parent gazes out
at tree-shapes spread like peacocks on
a lake (the town); at grass-loop shine;
at the empty lit set-up of this street.

And likes the way the paling fence below
is reclining into weeds. A thickened tree
by the house has its bole brush-swiped
with shadow. At this time the milkman came.
Now, the marching-girl flickers of TV.

A horse crops close around arc-lights'
twin metal poles, in the paddock next door,
that rise from concrete beside a car-yard
and make a light of grainy plastic there.
It's like a snapshot from a passing car.

Another way, the neon signs, and trees
rank as weeds; and the last, squeezed light,
beautiful and calm — as when illness emptied
her face. And you had thought, Why not
like this sooner? Why now, when it's too late?

Nine Bowls of Water

Clear water, in silvery tin dishes
dented as ping pong balls:
a lemon juice tinge of the staling light is in them;
they've a faint lid of dust.

A potted water along a board slopped
and dripping lightly.
While the men work on the city road, excavating
its charred blackness,

the water waits
behind a corrugated iron shed that is set

at the pavement front,
under the tall shadowing empty stadium.

On that low plank, also, crude soap pieces,
bright as the fat
of gutted chickens — but, with a closer look, resistant,
darkly-cracked, like old bone handles —

one beside each bowl,
and the rags are on their bits of hooked wire.
The cars continue,
but few people walk here between the lunch shed

and brick wall. Set out along a wet bench,
the kneeling water:
this reality from which we have dreamed the spirit.
We walk in grittiness,

on papers, mud-scrapings,
splattered with a sporadic jackhammer racket,
past nine bowls of water — a gallantry of the union.
Trees in avenues and sailing boats and women.

Under the Summer Leaves

1

Every morning we left the wooden hotel
and crossed the estuary along a footbridge,
that had some of its planks and lengths of rail missing,
going to the sandhills and surfing beach.
This bridge made a tilting, crooked line
through the tops of a mangrove swamp,
the round leaves of which were shining, green
as small tree frogs. Stepping from the long boardwalk
on the far shore, close to the river's flexed arm,
we found the water deepened after the bend,
blocked from the mangroves with a low breakwater,
and here it became a peacock's purplish-blue,

always fluttering in the seabreeze.
The jumbled stone breakwater running ahead of us dragged
a taut rein at the river's bending neck.
We walked on a track between the granite,
of waist-height, and the swamp trees
from out of black sand — those insect legs and torsos
of pandanus, and the mangroves, overlapping
so densely, they immediately obscured their reserve.
Small crabs were sprayed from our shadows backwards,
glaring stalk-eyed and showing open claws —
each was like a cricketer who reverse-pedals,
demanding 'Mine!' We'd look behind,
over the river's broad, slewed cornering,
and see the blue hotel — steep-roofed
as though the gaudy, watched-over descendant
of the indigo hills. Beside the hotel
was a fused mass of pines,
and this seemed to have drawn from out of those mornings
all of their sediment, all their darkness.

Then going on, into the heath, towards the green
vine-covered sandhills, on which slant
white paths were slashed — winding adrift, in high grass,
for the two hundred yards of a natural category.
A matt green and russet country, seemingly so drab,
that's of a texture more rich than all
the agricultural shows' embroidery stands.
The whitest sand, or salted grey sandstone, underfoot.
A few eucalyptus, wind-crook'd
and loosely splattered with leaves, are there,
flesh-white, unyielding; isolate
above a close detail from an Old Master — the smoky dark
and drips of rose madder and yellow ochre;
above those brushes, with their scumblings;
over the broomhead coarseness, the fur,
spines, horse-combs, pennants, and fine white flowers
that float, wind-borne, like splintered water.

For transcendence, we've the clouds of autumn,
the clouds of summer, that build plinth on plateau,
and then domes and cupolas, or billow
as though Renaissance draperies; modelled with a wash
and Tiepolo soft. One comes upon these best
across the dry heath of the Coast.

But first, each day, we'd have to pass
a last great complicated trunkless mangrove,
sprouting myriad-limbed off the earth,
and every time, a man would be standing in there,
amid its crooked mesh of shadows.
He remained very still, his back to the path
on which a few people walked —
the young boardriders, reluctantly returning,
lugging a short board against the hip,
their broad faces with a white stripe, sullen and stolid
like dripping steers; the shrill girls
keeping to their own groups, brown as a baker's shop, and carrying
radios long as suitcases, wispy salt afloat
above their shoulders, and on the foreshores of their chests;
and sometimes older people, going outwards,
unemployed fishermen, pensioners, wearing floral hats
and towels like astrakhan collars,
in their seaweed idleness.
That man was leaned slightly against a thick branch,
one hand propped along it, never glancing
as we came by. Although he was shaded with a lattice,
you could see he was an Aboriginal
by the hand from a sleeve, and the igneous bones
of the last quarter of his face.
There were bottles everywhere about his feet
but never any foodscraps or paper, nor signs of a camp.
An aurora of immense, pure, colourless light
would be vaulting upwards ahead of us
within an absolute shade of blueness; vaulting on itself
and upon itself

like the felt streamings of a gas flame,
from beyond the sandhills, and their grandstand view.

When I was growing up around there, that place had been
just another small town off the highway,
with mothy streetlights, a motel's insomnia,
tree-roots under the pavement blocks,
broken fences and long yards, white fibro
beyond the trees' broad shadows,
bougainvilleas, weatherboards.
Now there were split-level Spanish houses
in an estate across the hillslopes. There was the first
tall block of flats. Tourists were driving
to the beach, along the new road; and out there, you found,
was also getting freckled over.
Now the cars and motorbikes were everywhere,
their tyre-marks drawn about the sand
like great tangled ropes — so that people might seem
a lynch mob, threatening everything that's natural.
Technology both gives and removes us from the world —
hardly ever increases our ability to experience it;
rather, speed and ease mean uninvolvement,
and so condescension, remoteness, emptiness.

Each morning we'd stay in the surf for hours,
then lie at a slant among the sandhills
to watch the bumping approach of the ocean;
to hear the waves pile-driven,
and see the boardriders slip backwards from them.
We saw how, as those waves advanced, they'd disperse,
transversely, a running whiteness,
as though shed by a plough-share;
the whole rostered ocean, lifted upon its lifting,
would stall blue-green a second, and then fire
a white flare, to meet a similar trajectory
from further along its folding water,
before all was lost, on their collision,
in the complete collapse of the house;

in a white chaos,
as when a snow-laden pine tree is felled into deep snow.

That town, beyond the river bank, was now
a main street of brick shops, all
a contused dull red, and shaped like public lavatories,
but with advertising over the windows,
on the flat rooftops, along the awnings;
a place of thongs, and of shorts tilted under stomachs;
of loud cars making fast getaways,
then returning in a few minutes;
of poker machines, video porn, real estate agents,
and of pop music, wallowing from the wide supermarket,
with its leering or lachrymose imagery;
of tarry electric wires slung low across everything.
In the rowdy bars were the appetites
like a steel rod draped in flesh. We could see,
from the hotel's empty first floor verandah,
from that one old building that remained,
how people had come there out of the cities
and had built the packed suburb of the caravan park.
Some day there'll be nothing but urban men —
I imagined their lives as like that shuffling water,
tepid, brackish, and shallow,
over the sandbank in the silted river.

We used to go again to the sea of an evening;
the only ones to tire, it seemed,
of the pounding and clamour at the pub,
that was like the tugging of a bonfire,
in which you could feel their rage for more.
We'd find a cool breeze out there
after the narcotic afternoon,
and moonlight strewn on the green-black ocean
looked like a scattering of shaved ice.
We wondered if the Aboriginal was sleeping then
under his tree, or drinking alone,
but it was too dark to say, and we'd no wish

to interfere. We often spoke of him, casuistically,
'as the breeze sighs through the withered fern.'
All we guessed was, he must be a half-caste,
coming from there. Of a day, for nearly a week,
every time we went out to the ocean, and again no matter
how long we stayed, he'd be standing
in the wide tree that flung its branches
immediately off the sand. He occasionally took a sip,
and always looked in one direction, his hand lightly
on a bough — gazing over the suede,
buff-coloured reeds, above the low swamp trees,
and through a faint salt-dust in the air, towards,
or so it seemed (although probably he could hardly
     have seen
a thing), but if you followed his gaze,
towards a particular mountain, blue
and symmetrical, and stuccoed faintly
along its edges with a forest line; one that was stepping
forward, fluted, out of the range, and
that lifted to its node of satisfaction.
A mountain piled there as though it were something
trickled up on the pan of a scale.

2

This town we'd thought our holiday from the future.
We had come there after months in Japan —
back out of the tunnel Australia was entering.
From Tokyo, Osaka, Nagoya,
Kyoto and Hiroshima: those places of a constant smoke,
like bushfire days, of chemical stench, unending
     concrete;
cities run together, and superimposing on each other;
that people made seem, each, a shattered ants' nest.
In Japan, they have named the steep, unusable
     mountains
national parks (that are the calendar face
of their country), but had found a new use for them:

during our stay, a campaign had begun for blasting these,
so as to add to the country sideways.
The Japanese could do this.
Already they bulldoze the hills for lime,
to kerb and gutter the coast; and rivers are straightened
and lined with concrete, the word for which translates
'correcting' the river. And yet, they sentimentalize
on nature. Plastic autumn leaves are hung
from the light poles, in Tokyo's treeless streets.
The Japanese attitude really is,
'If its back points to the heavens, then eat it.'
Lift a plating off the live lobster's back
and take with chopsticks that wet porridge
while its fronds
counterpoint your controlled pick.
Nature is just an approved view.
At prescribed places on the Hokkaido highway
one has a prescribed response.
Though, now you must censor for yourself
the pylons, in swathes, all akimbo like armoured samurai,
the chimneys, or reactors, that jostle a relic —
those moss-padded rocks, and bamboos parted,
by a temple, that is hollow as a movie set. You will find
the camera's a fine pair of blinkers.

Nature manipulated, miniaturized is the preference
where earth and weather are so treacherous.
No one really cares there to live in the country:
a people of such centripetal impulse
they pack into cities, that are always
square-limbed and brutal as their printed *kanji* —
where nature is only the moon
(and not the air, certainly), fallen into a dust-grey sky
in summer, like a big rotting persimmon, or
in winter, on a dusk that is mauve and furry as a crystal,
a salt-white precipitate, at the bottom of a tube —
they pack into cities, and into those trains

that, if spruce, are only cattle trucks, and
as in their houses, keep all the windows closed in summer.

You begin to imagine things that might be done
by a country where so many
are still at their desks, when you pass on a lifting train
the ice-cube trays of office lights
toward midnight, and you learn
there they remain
until the overseer has decided to go home.

The Bomb's of more influence in Japan than the Buddha:
they have suffered power, and will now assert it.
(Though, the major tradition has long been the
    Confucianist,
with its utterly entangling obligations,
its narrowness of sympathy, its servilities.)
Buddhism is dead, like an empty crab shell —
except, there is something of the name, which is an inversion,
invented by a kind of Norman Vincent Peale.
A professor said to me, The things you admire
of the past (Ryokan's poems, restraint, rock gardens)
only belonged to an elite: it was they
who listened to bamboos, and the eaves dripping,
who viewed the moon, and wrote
poems for each other; they who could wander
from temple to temple, or stay in some grass hut
on their own. Ordinary people, in those times,
weren't allowed even a family name — they worked, they
    got drunk,
they'd the bath house, and the raucous theatre;
for them, the forest was closed and dim;
if you weren't, for instance, a diver then
(until Meiji, in 1860, or even until MacArthur),
then you had no business to swim.
Released by the capitalists, by their mode of production,
this class lacks a taste for the Japanese past.
They prefer *kitsch*. And their possessing it
so vastly — from Big Macs and Coca Cola

to plastic woodgrain and fluffiness to Mickey Mouse —
is all we can mean, when we say they are rich.

So my arriving there was a goodbye. And yet, for what
they contribute to Utopia, gratitude.
It was myself I had found, in their imagery.
Those polished long floorboards, which seem of a day
moonlit. The forests where a berry fell
onto a pool, and a white bird flew
in the dark halls. The bamboo flute, lifting to wander
as a crane's wings. And Zen masters like Dōgen, who when he
    dipped
water from a stream, in the bamboo dipper,
poured half back, before he would drink, since
he felt all things as interdependent.
Now there are others, who believe themselves humbled
in their own faces, and in front of the lank-voiced Americans,
before all 'red-faced and merely physical
Westerners', and these grasp at things,
but without the room, and so they have potential
like turbine waters, stashed downwards
in darkening strata,
and growing heavier. And yet, they also must see
how just outside their always low-burning, respectful light
all the qualities beyond mechanism
have blown away, fast
as smoke-shapes over grass.
Their lives are in all human ways
much worse than these in the loose-end-of-town cities
of the world, the Australian cities. Free trade,
no doubt, will sell us to their obsessions:
to that religion, the one Japanese family; to the demands
of a mask, that are cruel as lacquer.

Although the purpose of travel is homesickness
I achieved this too soon in Tokyo —
a city where only warehouses face the water.
When I saw this I knew
that for all my love of things in their culture,

and though I'd received there much formularized
    kindness,
it is with *Die Natur*
that my loyalties are.

One late night in Tokyo, when I was walking
near where I stayed, in a working-class district,
I felt the back-lane streets
all around me, stickily as a web, and saw them, as if
    from above,
tight like the crazing on a glaze.
The tram wires were tangled great molasses strings,
hung in a fast, low steam. The few small trucks
and quiet cyclists flowed quickly
into those dark capillaries. And then, for minutes,
a bubble stillness. No one seemed about, and yet I knew
there were people everywhere,
close by, behind the old wood and oil paper. I went on
more deeply, and came up to the fine, cold smirk
on the face of a fox god, above oranges
and incense, in a shrine at a dim corner.
The dishcloth sky was wrung of its few stale drops.
I was in a dense forest: wall to wall houses,
each of them three paces wide, adobe-shaped, of
    concrete,
deal planks and bamboo. Above all that,
on the low purple clouds, so lurid and cinematic,
there was more: blocks of flats,
all thirty stories, and slung of a day with futons and
    washing,
but that night only some lights,
like computers left on, in their obscure rank on rank.
And shadows of smoke hove across these;
smoke still rolling out of the factories — in the cold air
becoming as dense and deeply-gathered
as the wool of a ram's neck; and this was being added
to the bales always piling there.
Then I came to a closed market street: a place
I had seen with its stalls open,

amid the bicycles' chrome occlusions. A usual
Asian market, all steam and broken-toothed screeching,
the forearms complicit in skewerings,
those barrels of flensed squid, protoplasmic,
and vegetables sinking through the spectrum of rot.
That night in the silent, flushed-out street
the closed fish stall was rank
like a raw, coarse smell of ocean —
so that I saw at once a long jetty, out of my boyhood's
foolishness. One I used to clamber underneath,
self-testing, of a night; coming back
from its far end, along a charcoal-black, slippery
calligraphy, until the night I fell,
had fallen, into the ragged, freezing salt-solution
that burned at my skin
and the filigree membranes inside my head. And there,
baptised in shock, I'd felt myself kidnapped
one-handedly, transferred
on a big swell,
out into the emigrant harbour; dangling
my legs in a steel lift-well. I saw
across a smoky beach, and empty dunes, the streetlights,
weakly blue, and the top floors of the hotel,
bulged with light; and heard,
as with a faulty memory, bits of what
the dance band played. I knew myself alone
with a sea-diluted voice;
where I seemed to have forgotten
how, even, to get out of my jacket. And I'd a sort of vision
     there,
for a moment, of the dining room table at home
as my plate was being removed.

And then I was remembering Japan,
above the bright estuary, in a hotel room.
Gauze curtains were blowing in the wardrobe mirror,
there was sand on the lino, swim trunks
hung from the door, and the loose holiday crowd
was outside, the thong-flapping Australians,

flickering or yelling, through the enormous light.
And I saw we are much as the Japanese are —
all 'determined by the means of production';
the same machines, or machine-profferments,
allure us, and have shaped us all.
We're all sentimentalists of a Millennium,
who cannot conceive there is wealth in not having.

Every afternoon of our holiday it would rain —
how it comes down
on that part of the Coast, for about an hour,
from almost exactly 3.00, in the summer.
Under a dense, potato-shaped cloud,
with its black loam, its nightshade tinge of green,
a hair-root is suddenly struck.
And in the west, along a compressed zone
of aniseed tint, there's an urgently-running cardiogram.
The light dims for a matinee,
and clouds are dilated in the shape of bellowing;
then rain flies like a silvery train,
and there are long rumblings, as though a bridge upheld it.
All the country grows loose in the rain.
I had a front seat, out by the railing,
and onto that gloom would leap
the wonderful high look
of the wings of Samothrace, whenever the banana trees
    were lit.
It would end too soon,
with long drips as in a water tank;
with a creaking and shuffle on the tin roof
lightly, like Fred Astaire.

Once, after the rain, I walked from town,
by the seedpod fences, along the rammed earth of a road
on which double tyre-marks shone
far into the cellular afternoon. And the road shone again
in ellipses toward the hills.
The sun had come back, carrying its skirts
among the trees; and so I turned

in there, onto a track. Every leaf poised its medicine drops.
The ivory paddocks gleamed
beyond fire-blackened stringybarks
that had the texture and sheen of crushed velvet.
The lily pads shone
on a swamp of tobacco brown —
those shapes out of which the frogs are inflated.
A long-fronded, elated afternoon.
There was a rhythm among the saplings from Tom Roberts,
and paperbarks that Nolan has taught us to see.
I came out on a hillslope above the lilac ocean.
Light on the clouds opposite sunset
was like that in the foyer of a seashell.
White eucalyptus rose about me in front of the sea, their leaves
long like green parakeets.
The mind easily fragments within such dimensions: I felt it poise
far above, a second, as I was leaning
there, on the moist, thin rind
which is all that is delicacy, all that's edible fruit,
of this country. Then I realized how probably the land
I had just walked over was already owned
in some boardroom of Hong Kong or Japan. And all I'd just seen
became things that lay in a fire
in the moment when they still have their form.

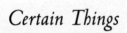

Certain Things

Currawongs

Dinner-jacketed, these birds stroll like the mafia, to air
their respectability.
Our acquaintance long made, it seems they've assumed we couldn't
    care
about amorality.

They'll bring the peeled-looking nestling, to eat it on our clothes
    wire,
where we have offered them bread;
have often chosen to chuck down here the cellophane wrapper
and the moulded plastic head

of cicadas. One slowly ate a silhouetted grasshopper,
lifting it in a fanfare;
stylised with pride, as though it were holding a broken swastika.
They have tightly brushed-back hair,

snipy Latin features, an expression like a thin moustache,
but the eye is demonized
and belongs more to an African carving, than to an *apache*.
The eye, barely capsulized

in its split pod, has a rind of poisonous yellow around
a blackly-shining, opaque
blight. It is watching every movement in the air, on the ground,
as if it's all a card-stake.

Such birds live more intensely than any gangsters on the run.
Although, at times they deploy
with police cars' confidence — another role they have taken on —
sounding their *calloy, calloy*,

c'loy, a siren, ordering the neighbourhood. On the grass
they appear to strut with arms
slightly akimbo, and with the sense of limited nimbleness,
the stumpiness, and what seems

the cocky, tilted head, alert for notice, of the bodybuilder.
And then, a pin-pointing beak
is applied quickly, intently, while they stare like a welder.
I noticed one had grown weak,

in the park, below our railing. Through the summer afternoon
it stood drowsily about,
although wary, and when at last the darkness had sifted down
it died, by leaping out,

suddenly, beneath the only headlights in some while on
      our street,
confused, at the last minute.
That most resonant thump, of something live; and also,
      I thought,
crunch of bird-twigs. I found it

still breathing, horribly; the beak split wide, and held by a
      thread,
as happens when wood is splayed,
the eyes squeezed hard, without lashes or tears. It was crash-
      landed,
crumpled. I ran for a spade;

and answered, 'Don't come,' while disentangling the blade in the
      dark;
returned, to find it was gone —
and saw two boys, holding something on the far side of the park,
who looked behind as they ran.

God no, I thought — they'll poke about, then toss it into a
      lane,
soon bored, or over a fence
to a dog, and cackle and run on, already with some new plan. . . .
Those birds are their most intense

at twilight, in scalloping flight, against the horizon's fire-coal
orange, where it tilts a ramp
onto indigo. They'll strictly show and close the wing's porthole
like a signalman his lamp.

There are some admire them, who admire what remains them
     in us,
who admire the deed, *elan*,
health, affirmation; but now what I see, also, is the pathos
of braggarts and the strong.

At dusk, stepping beneath the drawn latex of vast grey fig trees,
the wolf-whistling currawongs;
or scoring across harbour sails, that are stretched like beer bellies;
above waves' slap, listless as thongs.

Harmonica

The lamps came on
along the platform, all of them round as dandelion heads
in the sea-mist.

We heard the sea,
from behind a corrugated iron shed, trudging
with Sisyphus tread.

A few of us waited
on that empty stage, way out of town.
The train was late.

There was an Aboriginal; a pair
of old hippies were talking tough in the eighties;
a man and woman arrived, country types.

The town, across the heath,
might have been some lights of a freeway; the road to there
a trickle, in sandy scrub.

The man and woman hardly spoke:
boots, jeans, sheepskin collars; his balding head;
hers the luggage, in plastic bags.

She wore his hat; he'd had a drink.
A middle-aged girl with loose open face, the sort
who might come on a bumpy road.

She waited calmly, in the cold.
He took out and began quietly working on
harmonica, and wasn't bad.

Tapping his boot. A melancholy,
pure and steady, was unwound along the night
a little way.

He knew the great songs, like 'Irene';
the last was 'Amazing Grace'. We'd drawn a bit closer
in the wind.

But kept to the wavering
edges of his tunes. It was private. That sort of thing
hardly happens in an airport lounge.

The train simply appeared, its sound
blown away. A single light, sliding around the forest,
like a satellite out from its planet.

His last address to her,
which I could hear, as she stepped up, was the part
     about
'... that saved a wretch

like me. I once was lost, but now I'm found;
was blind,
but now I see.'

'The Pines'

I went from the town on foot, as seemed fitting for a pilgrimage;
going in the way that we used to, down a white road on the gravel
 verge.

The sunlight came from amongst the tall eucalyptus with a
 censer's swing.
Although nearly forty years later, imagining I could find
 something.

Even now, there were only a few cars, that passed by at a wave.
I arrived before the great wall of pines, and through its black
 architrave

were the slant paddocks, steaming with weed-tops in the
 afternoon light.
What I am is that earth, towards the mountains, made animate.

And I found there now a real Hell's Kitchen of the vegetable
 world —
every kind of trash that grows; lantana and stinking roger
 run wild;

wolfish leaves with deceiving white hairs, their splintery stings;
blackberry ramping; all the nonsensical, stickily-branching
 things.

The place had been bulldozed, and grass was overcome, grey and
 thin,
by farmer's friends (my trousers, the caricature of a bristled chin);

by scrawled plants, equivalents of limpet and slug, in a furtive
 strife;
things sordid as on a sludgy coastline the cockroachy
 crustaceous life.

  I sat on the ground, among grass plumes, to tell myself the
   sad story

of the death of a king, although was fitfully dissuaded from
    being sorry

by a long sceptre of the sunlight that was tilted again
    towards me;
by glimpsing, amid rabble, the maroon, ivory, and tawny-gold
    livery

of the true grass of childhood, and through a light golden as
    Avalon
the hills, still sharp-peaked, as an old log that's been idly hewn.

Below those hills, retracting promontories of eucalypt forest,
    with a seed-head
foliage, mistily, and the tight fleece, hiding the river, clumpy
    and fissured.

I'd hoped to see again the marvellous clouds that accumulate
    upwards there
and make a brilliant Gondal — its every inlet, mountain, and
    peninsula.

Could anyone have loved a place more than I did this one,
as a fair-haired boy? Beneath the silver-laden tree of the dawn,

within the rotunda of days, the wind-polished immensities
    of heaven,
amid simmering herbs, plaited water, my spirit was as empty
    and clean.

It was all physical, I think: not the soul, but the nervous
    system;
the subtleties of a young animal; and the chosen aloneness,
    and freedom.

I turned to find the house, going waist-deep toward the
    Moreton Bay fig tree,
its silver blight like photographs of the moon's scars. Only
    the chimney

showed, of that wreckage, which was wrapped in vines and
    shooting rubbish;
out of bamboo and sour leaves, nettles, and the canes with spines
    like fish.

I'd wandered through many days in that house, confined to a dim
    bedroom,
in daydreams. And could see myself again, a girl to what I have
    become,

who only wanted to push there, though torn; to find something
    and hack
to my own side, and to kiss those lips, and make my heart awake.

Travelling

High up in the hotel
the sound of traffic, at noon,
troubling
as water left to boil.

•

An early train,
when the streets are washed down.
Office buildings among the clouds, billboards,
blown grass.

•

Telegraph poles, splattered
ink of tree-tops,
and always
the falling
frothy river
of the sky.

•

Wandering late
among a myriad lit
shop windows, with rain
afloat. Those deep

reflections lifting you
onto catwalks.

●

Sunlight comes low
across the bars
of fences, and among
the corn leaves;
it makes a fox terrier pattern
on dirt roads, and is trying
openly
with its final cast
for a fisherman
on the windy river.

●

A whinge of rapid pigeon wings, as
fan-dancing
they descend, out of morning light.
The cornice is a compote
that only wants to rot.

●

On a train, through the long summer evening,
beneath a Wedgewood landscape.
The dark girl's eyes
are lost,
sealed like cowrie shells.

●

All day the clouds: some of them milk
discharged onto a river,
others
timber planed against the grain.

●

On the paddocks, a trudging afternoon —
the smoke disaffections,
shadows claimant.

●

A long walk, which leads to a bare
suburban street,
among empty lots,
where the palings are left to stand
in afternoon storm-light.

●

Below the sandhills
a man goes jogging, on his tough small
reflection, that wriggles
like the heart —
the exuberance
of someone who is treading
his own grapes. The surf
is a mural of Valhalla. A dog, all
wet strings, flaps behind
him, its barking
distant timber thrown down. This
beneath a sky of swept
charcoal, an ocean
in strata
of graphite and silver.

●

Two boys are hanging out
from the cold ladder
of a reservoir
at dusk, and pointing to a heron
that floats away
across the heath, over
the tips of all
the orange grass.
The movement of that bird's wings
is like the waving
of the long grass
in the breeze.

●

From a train, the traveller sees
at first light,
far across the fields, against the foreshortened
slate-blue ocean,
a white lighthouse.

The Girls

All those unbalanced galaxies —
their rivets splayed,
the gas-blue constrictions.

And across the playing fields
lies a blue-white mist
of arc-lamps.

There are girls at practice,
implacable strike
of their hockey sticks,

whose limbs surpass
anything we have contrived
in wood, for shapeliness.

Wandering the pavements,
I watch with the separate men
through wire-netting

the girls play exactly
where they may, within a silent
roaring, and fangs of light.

Nothing seems so marvellous
as a small white ball
exchanged among their sticks.

In Thin Air

for Dee

It's songs of you that they play
while I eat alone
the grease of one more café
in an overnight town;

but the arrangements are all made,
the paperwork's done,
and the money has been paid,
so I'm going on —

a swimmer who can't climb
the high stone walls
or a boat ramp, for the slime,
as night falls.

I'll have to go much further
before turning home.
There's kindness of a stranger;
the best is long known.

Icicles, knobbly as candlewax,
that's long on bottles
or hung from candlesticks,
along the hotel lintels,

where I say your name to ingots
on purple night; to steam
above a few houses; to overcoats,
women inside, blown home.

The snow is shapely as meringue,
thousands of miles to come. . . .
I have done such things too long.
Tips of obelisks in foam,

as we came by, were cemeteries;
a river, grey-veined marble;
the mauve, frozen smoke of trees;
snow smothering every gable.

A corruption is waiting hidden,
Conrad somewhere said,
even for affection so freely given
as ours; much is paid.

I lie in the long midnight train.
Thickly, black pinions fly;
we howl in a forest like wolverine.
Dawn's weird chemical sky.

Then most of the day, keeping on
through Canada, I forget
the book I am reading, well begun,
because of looking out —

to wet black trees, snow-sprayed
one side (as if arc-lamp
lit), all of them fraying, then frayed;
to lakes, cold fat on soup;

to a young woman, who was in snow
and steam we'd driven,
standing at nightfall to see us go
at a forest stop, on her own.

Plain houses, of doors and windows;
calcified silos, stables.
Out here, occasional light shows,
early, and warm as waffles.

Morning puts its tongue in the lock,
kisses an iron door, draws away
the lips, leaving blood. How quick
a passion, corroding all the sky. . . .

In the Rockies, one's enthusiastic:
Sunsets built of stone.
I thought of that haiku, 'A firefly, look!
Forgetting I was alone.'

There was a waterfall at full stint,
frozen to its rock,
like quartz, or a stroke of paint.
Stopped again, I'm taking stock.

It seems that I've gone far enough
to be offered normal life,
as though flipping over a disc.
I'd never thought to ask.

My life, I imagined, must be a hymn
to the optic nerve.
Other senses, you have proven,
will have all they deserve.

The Room

A round table-top
with a bowl of fruit,
and a black merchant ship

far behind it;
with the peaches' russet nap
and a yellow crescent

lightly speckled.
The cloth's blue and white
diagonals make

a stylized net
of clouds, on this altar
to the Altering —

before the convolvulus
mountains, the
daubed mackerel sky,

the hazy light
of the sidelong bay.
A breeze in here,

as though we heard
a pure note
on the ocean's single string.

A Testimony

Gloomy midnight in spring, rain sinking on the canes in the
    garden. I wanted some ease
from my confusion, and reached out through lamplight for a
    pen.

I am one of those who have watched their image in the hearth,
    where a fire
was tearing itself into pieces, with its nails and with its fists.

And when shall I lie again in a landscape that is bright like
    satin
with my Venus of the sweet grass, her breasts as plump as quail?

Shall we sing hymn three six six: 'Art thou weary, art thou
    sad?' As though it matters,
for who are we? Blowing in the abyss, these crying-out shapes
    of smoke.

The one perfection of this world is lust: is grasping, scheming,
    longing. And entirely of nature,
we're continuous with whatever binds the faceless pebble, that
    more truculently persists.

Along the bladed mountains, and in the deep ravines, flow-
    ers come forth unknown to men
and pass away unseen. When it is spring there, a thousand
    bloom. Why should this be, and for whom?

Existence must come of itself, and it goes on and on with-
    out a reason, just because it is.
In human consciousness, it produced an eye. It has arrived
    where it might understand. Perhaps it cannot bear this.

We have envied the crane, her clear bright wings out-
    stretched in fear, that flees the dark stormcloud,
seeking a shelter, and to safe shelter, to all her shelter borne.

We have envied when we thought how in the morning light,
    gently outpoured as from a tin,
that awakens Asia's folds, some dusty marauder puts out its
    claw and retakes the earth.

For us, all is whirled away and is vanishing, as though it
    were the sparks of a trampling flame.
Something comes into existence if it coheres with other
    things; but this everlasting fire lives on fire, on all of
    itself.

Difference, which is loss for us, is the life of matter. And
    without an opposing force, each thing would cease to be.
'Strife is the natural state; it is the source of all. The oppo-
    sites are in agreement, as in a drawn bow.'

The first philosophers were the best, as well as briefest.
    'Everything is metamorphosis, and nothing can remain.'
    How could men have dreamed
that they would impose their demands upon the nature of
    this world?

There is a substance to things, which is ungraspable,
    unbounded; divided and passed on, like a secret
    inheritance; always present, in what is always passing, but
    never found in itself — it both is and is not.

Thus matter is profound; is *potentia*. And all that now exists is
   like the surface of the waters.

Things as they are are what is mystical. Those who search deep-
   est are returned to life,
to ferns in a jug on the window-ledge, to a burned-off hillslope
   in the dusk that is like an opal.

To a spirited horse, chrysanthemums, a pannikin that drips,
   creeping vines, a cut, the corners
of the mouth, a bedspread, willows, the bowels, shadiness, a
   lump, bright salad, and dust above distant fields.

We are given the surface again, but renewed with awe. And I
   remember what I have to say:
Do not believe those who have promised, in any of their ways,
   that something can be better than the earth.

Although I say this with grief for all of those beings who are like
   shuffling, lumpy birds within a basket,
where they have spent or will spend their lives, and my heart feels
   suddenly stunned.

Again, as in a lit cavern, the headland's crumbling silhouette, the
   wind's emery paper glitter,
the serrations of the bay. And the paddocks, dipping into the sea.

Now a blossom slips through the tall wet boughs that are
   speckled with flowers. Beneath them, and above the hillslope's
   other trees,
out on the ice-pale harbour, one of the yachts begins its drifting
   away.

Again, the dog is dancing on the morning dew. This black dog
   that will drape itself like an odalisque
amid the jacaranda's mauve shadow, at noon. That can make us
   seem a sickness of the apes.

What is most needed is that we become more modest. And the
    work of art that can return us to our senses.
Our only paradise is the ordinary: to be fed by what is really
    here.

Now the sea is dark and harsh as shale. The afternoon storm, a
    swamp growth; sluggish bubbles,
above the whiteness of lawn bowls, on the small town's freshly
    painted green.

Looking out, from a verandah in the forest edge, onto tin roofs,
    drive-ins, supermarkets, fishing boats,
the ocean slopping by the tea-shops, and the coarse
    cheese-rind of the beach.

In the smoky skirts of a brilliant immensity, the headland is
    sleeping like a paw. There, pine trees are shaped as though
    ink blotted
in the folding of a page. From out of those diffusing hills, an
    empty wet highway's light swallow play.

That road falls to offices and banks, to three spires (with their
    wrongly-directed penitence).
Now, the bunches of the tree-tops are rolling; a white sail has
    gone. Slant rain.

In late afternoon, I read on the verandah, and then look at the
    clear dusk. A striped towel hangs across the rail, beside the
    banana palms.
A single wing on the tall sea is passing the continents of the
    moon.

The West

The grey sheep are bundles
of grass coiled
and blown tottering, trundled
a little way, in hot wind.

The grass here is born as straw.
Grey-haired bush,
sparse and low, has been scrubbed in
with a tatty brush.

Mostly, there are sticks with hooks,
then stains,
scratches, specks — the flaws
in the weathered canvas of the plains.

We crawl the bottom of a reservoir
that is filled with light *ad infinitum*.
On the salt pan, the light is pure
as milked venom.

One only drives fast through this,
as though with lungs desperate to ascend.
The surface is the narrow strand
of the coastland.

There appear rarely
the improvised strange contraptions
of the trees —
they are like crazy antennae,

standing by the blue tar
of the road, which is full of sky
in long shoals;
or they're land yachts, with riddled sails

of brown or olive-grey,
that lopsidedly blow
toward us; or in a group, they're the shotgun wreck
of an old shanty's fibro.

And the tall leaning silver trucks
with black-goggled faces,
that rupture the sacs of the air,
leave tangled meat as spore —

those Francis Bacon emblems
on the conveyor belt. Their hunger
exhales on the car
as, tall as a clipper or a circus van,

they come floating, then stand
and rush on us like sharks
that leave the sea — out of the mirage's
stylized water,

with their camouflage sheets
abandoned, they strike
right beside us, blind. They are about all
you see here of humankind.

It is a landscape that seems stepping back
through the light, out of what is real,
like the one in a photograph
that was left on a windowsill.

Wintry Evenings

How beautiful the girls are
of a rainy winter's evening, with legs in warm stockings,
    so tenderly solicitous of themselves:
        small shoulders
      in coats, and the hair brushed out
before leaving work, ceremoniously, upon their shoulders.
    Those legs are like a waterbird's, in quick quick
        transposings
      against lights of the traffic,
stepping silhouetted as though along a causeway, over
    the road that is a dredged lip of molten ore.
        And they pass
      alleys that rot like swamps, that
are dripping with the obscene mantras of rainforests, but
    arrive, a skittering of ballerinas,
        feet swung out,
      safely within this awning.
There is the roundness of a small head above a tweed collar,
    like a bud — one has alighted near, her coat
        lapels stir
      at her breath, crooked fibres
laden with finest dew, as the black, bony tree close by
    a streetlight wears, in its great spiderweb form,
        a springtime
      of crystalline fruit. Traffic
moves like water that's almost level, trickles a little,
    congeals, and gathered nudges itself further
        along this
      avenue, beneath the high-
shouldered forms that it seeks to elude, it seems, amid steam.
    Those monoliths are inlaid with brazen plaques,
        which are here
      tropical cages the young
women sidle beside, their nostrils drawn even finer. They're
    awed by great art, the names within these panes;
        this is to them
      discovery rich as parchment.

The girls are lost to us, in the innocent arrogance
　　of their pleasure. But before the florist they
　　　　　turn again,
　　　　stagey on the pavement, glance
for the bus, with leather satchel strap drawn taut, gripped by
　　the small bird of the glove (that is branch-shifting
　　　　　and sudden,
　　　　fluttering and alighting
and darting away, among lilt and shrillness). Heads shiny
　　as seeds, waists like an otter, the girls with eyes
　　　　　dazzled by
　　　　a cogwheel jumble of drizzle
on eyelashes arrive, tilt the heads before chrysanthemums —
　　the pensive sweet lolling and the draped limbs of
　　　　　their bedspread
　　　　clowns. Although, one sits apart
on the bus stop bench, her gaze adrift in the water at
　　her feet, with an empty lap composing the
　　　　　Pietà
　　　　of all this dissolving world.
May she, in poor shoes, frail paper boat, never be taken up
　　by anyone with hands that are less tender
　　　　　than my own.

Descent

　　　　A white sail that is sharp
　　　　as a sabre tip
　　　　veers away, beyond the spire
　　　　in the headland's shape,

　　　　and like a sword is shone,
　　　　as the car slips down
　　　　towards the bay
　　　　of a late afternoon.

It's the sail that's alone
with which I'm taken,
in the back of this car,
sunset coming on —

the one that seems to shun
others' congregation,
although walking there
in the fields of Heaven.

Malthusian Island

Paradise is always within walls; here it is in the hotel grounds,
   or around some few great bungalows, with their gardens
   and pools. Outside, there is wide purgatory.

But within these places one finds a hospital's tenderness in
   the measuring of a drink. This is done by men of oiled
   wood, in white skirts stiff as paint: by these simply-whit-
   tled men, who can move their limbs without a creak, but
   whose heads begin to wobble if you speak to them, as
   though their necks were loose axles. It is their diffidence,
   the duffers, a lack of confidence, and it disconcerts, dis-
   parages us who cause it.

We attend a fervid religion in this island — all day, the censer
   and small bell come to hand, of the cocktails, giving thanks.

There is a melancholy in such heat, when you can do nothing
   except be waited upon, and yet the sweat runs down like
   water on sluiced panes, as though it were earned with the
   hardest work.

And there are the hundreds upon hundreds of crows, that at
   twilight rise above the old tiles, the Portuguese-style roofs
   of the town, silently, as if whole bonfires of charred newspaper had burst in the wind.

In the long twilight, a few saris come out to walk on the dusty, closely-grassed walls of the town, which was once a Portuguese, and then a Dutch, and then an English, fort: on these brown-blanketed ramparts that overlook the dust-pale, empty sea.

Each woman, as though the Virgin, comes stepping upon a private, unravelling, perpetual small cloud. But she brings her black listless drench of hair, her purple gums, the sphincter-colouring of her mouth, an anxious cunning, her sadly cunning innocence.

There is an English hedgerow tune from the clocktower above the town, on the stifling day's pale, steamy sky. No ironies here, though; no such luxuries. 'This is Paradise,' the old men smile erodedly and say. And with the sun, the deep grime, the damp rot, it does seem, at least, that life here will never end.

'Ah, Paradise,' they tell you, for a few coins, with flies on the cracked lips and on the heavy, beetle-casing eyelids. 'Is it not so, sir?' with much wobbling of the head they say.

The Indian is the emptiest ocean. Over the low wall, while at the roof-top swimming pool, you see the ocean has the pool's colour; with nothing, nothing there; no craft, not even a cloud (maybe a tanker, rarely, just within the horizon). There are usually just the crows, flying near, like a few scouts that openly deploy.

A Hindu lubriciousness is insinuated everywhere: in the decorations on houses and temples; in the shapes of the public buildings, which above the first floor are only ornamental flat façades, of a crumbling poor concrete — everywhere this facile, slippery curvaceousness. Inside, those places are bare, and dank as an old change-room's cement.

At the Catholic cathedrals there are Mary and Jesus and open
arms and ruby hearts and eyes thrown upwards and neatly
combed beards and long sceptres of light. Then, for relief,
one finds the Hindus' entirely unsentimental gods, which
are as gods would be. For the Hindus, a god is the typhus
bacilli; or it is the collector of skulls, that are worn strung
on the hips, as dry as gourds: the one who treads with
ornate smirk, and an oily pointing of the toe, on a child,
that is shrieking the world's great zero.

The Hindu temple has all over it carved figures, in a blurry
worn cement, that seem to writhe up there like maggots, in
the heat. An almost naked priest shows you inside, down
into a urinous damp, and in the dripping darkness holds up
his lamp, to the gods in their lairs. These are venomous-
looking as snakes in glass cases, or like big cats withdrawn
into their pits; and he hisses 'Kali' at your ear in the dark,
or 'Ganesh', of the elephant-faced one, with its penis trunk
and body like a scrotum, and its sly, slit, mascaraed eyes.

A relief, to visit the educational Buddhists, at their stupa,
their Big Meringue, that is painted a plastery pink, blue,
and white. There, you see the vast and bland-faced statue,
with its matronly, gracious gesture; and murals of people
who are always sitting about, being taught, in pastels. It is
like the socialist version of a Sunday school. The Buddha
wears light blue robes, a light smile, and his figure in the
pictures of him reclining for *parinibbana*, for his extinction, is
propped on one elbow, mildly, like someone who watches of
an afternoon the children's games. As though it were deliber-
ate, this image is the very opposite of a crucifixion. Outside,
the hopelessness of those lives. Buddhism is the perfection
of such hopelessness. And yet, which of us will not lose all,
whose situation not be a hopeless one?

A gardenia petal moon. The sound of a billiard break, amongst
the moon-soaked pulpy flesh of night. In the garden,
frangipani petals and giant cockroaches flop onto the warm
swimming pool.

Nothing really differs from the days of the Raj. There are the servants and the foreign waited-on masters. Except, the foreigners now are more idle, and have less involvement. Perhaps they have less manners; certainly, they've less style.

In the first smoky-grey light, a few streetlamps still burn, and there is a pineapple tone out on the grey sea. All that moves is a dog, nosing about in deep shade, where a great tree is lightly blown. Then the dog goes on, and of course it is a three-legged one. There is a stir of refuse and rot, and the stiff-limbed stroll of a sheet of arse-wiping newsprint.

On all the signs, and in the soot-coloured newspapers the Sinhalese alphabet teems like spirochaetes. It writhes on the paper money, that is turning to mud. Long afterwards, there is a stench in that wallet as of filthy socks. Here, money literally stinks.

Standing packed and sweltering in a train, we travel often just metres from the sea, with its lightly-fluttered short fringe of foam. There are chicken-coop-sized huts, that have rotting grass tops, jostled wherever there is sand right out upon it. (The people here are almost equally spread all through the island's coastal undergrowth, and the cities are not more notable for their crowds. Everywhere, there is a crowd, or can be. If you stop your taxi on a dirt track in the jungle at night, people materialise all about, within minutes, barefooted, and angular as wood.) From the train you see, crowded down the coast, the long trunks of palm trees, lifting outward from here, like the slightly undulant vapour trails of jets, in a short surge, before the impulse explodes.

The train's sound underneath us is a tangled, thrashing metal. Then it seems to fall into talk about the places that we have seen. Katunayabe, Katunayabe, Trincomalee, Trincomalee, Mannar, Mannar, Chilewa, Mannar, Chilewa, Mannar, Trincomalee, Trincomalee, Belihul, Belihul, Belihul, Mannar, Belihul, Mannar, Belihul, Belihul, Trincomalee, Trincomalee, Trincomalee. . . . It is like the rushed and to us easily hysterical syllables of an Indian-style speech.

The heat has produced a continuous sullen smouldering or
  cloudiness of the light. There is a sickly, ubiquitous smell
  as if spicy food has burned black in the pot. Many of the
  buildings make together mouths full of decayed teeth; or
  they are flat-faced, low, and give a dull flat look onto the
  pebbles of the street, among which each day the shallow
  puddles come and go. And the people are like an acrid
  black smoke, adrift in the land.

The elephants on the road look so wilted they are each a
  caricature of someone slumping, in need of a cup of tea.
  They are led to the filthy river to bathe by young boys who
  are thin as sticks. You watch an elephant stepping down
  slowly, one corner at a time, that seems to have painful
  bandaged legs, and heavily stone-tipped feet; and it stands
  leaning forward on its trunk, and will only douse itself
  wearily, a throwaway gesture, with that outhouse stench,
  after it has been given many a shout, and clout. Mostly it
  just stands tilted from the bank, looking down, while the
  broad sludge turns into a copper screen behind it, and the
  palms and thatched huts of the other bank are smeared
  across with the smoky dark. A few tall birds come and sit
  on poles in the way that each boy sits, who has climbed up
  with the help of a tail onto his elephant's potato shape and
  is now hunched and folded there; and all of them watch
  how the oxide of the evening is slowly and blindly acting.

A white beach is ablaze in the morning, when we drive down
  the coast, and is such a pure and empty ellipse that we tell
  the taxi driver to leave us there and to come back late. The
  place is only crowded with palm trees, blindly enquiring
  for the horizon like tentacles. But the water is of blood
  temperature, and its bright greenness quickly comes to
  seem like that of a soft drink, it is so sticky. And where we
  sit down first is beside a coil of human crap. Young men
  soon come sidling up to sell us coconuts, which they lop
  the tops from with quick machetes, so that we can drink;
  and having satisfied a need they move on to dope, and for a
  time keep on and on, turning the conversation around
  again to dope, but finally see they must give up, and so

then they want to take us to the island in their canoe. But what island is that? There is none. 'Oh yes! Oh yes, sir! There it is, sir!' They point, and we shade our eyes, and see a quarter of a mile out, where the ocean is chrome-plated, a small lengthwise outcrop, very low in the water, of pitted rock. It is crinkled as cold lava, and the colour of rust, and striped all over with bird lime. Their canoe of driftwood is just along from here, tilted on the sand. 'There is the island,' they tell us. 'There it is. Come along, sir.' This is more farcical than a pantomime. We turn away from them, and see the 'island' again, easily now. They are silent, too. There doesn't seem anything we can say.

Doodling

The rain's
unbottled glut
is cluttering
in the porch's
corner. These
tight and blatherskite
convictions
of the rain.
A pearly fog
above the path's
diagonal
on the saturate
park, and that
sad industry
of crickets
is in recession
once again.
Distant streetlights
tremble, watery
emeralds; the cigar-
bright ember
of a slipping car.

Blue trees
are broad and scoured
like ink-blots;
and, exiled revellers,
each palm,
in bedraggled
feathery head-dress,
is forlorn
as a Fellini
mannequin.
At day's end
still amid desk work,
so the heavy
pile will sidle;
now, however,
I am idle.
There is always,
there is still,
that lit
window, the far
centre
to this one;
as if it were
an ending
to the corridor,
as though
that were here,
within space
and windy time.

The White Roads

On the deck
of an old fishing boat

I saw gulls slowly walk
and sparrows hop

that tipped
briefly as a pepper pot,

and far from the dunes
through the galleries

of mulberry trees
of an afternoon

I watched the swallows
roll and float.

On South Head

The shouts of workmen at football through the twilight
from these wide, elsewhere-empty playing fields
as I walk at their wet perimeter. And the South Head light
again dumps flour on the players, and congeals,

in my head only, their stretching attitudes —
crackles their movements like static — has moved on
above a vague, cement-stiff ocean, while it extrudes
itself, quickly as a cat snatching, on the horizon.

The slingshot trajectory of that snowball flight
compacts into the furthest smoke-wall, without trace;
resumes, stiffly as a white cane, around half the night,
over youths, Laocoön for each other, on this high place,

within a wire fence along the clifftops; swinging over
water-plump lawns, rounded to their brutal deficit;
and, far off, a phantom regiment of rain. Patchy as clover,
the sea below, with mine-deep sounds. In the opposite

direction, a deep elision of the landscape has banked
the city behind the players and a rickety tall goal —
stumps, fire-beaded, on a burned hillslope. This is flanked
by purple cloud and luminous plasma. And lights trail,

a long stream of sparks, amid the city's gouts of light.
Matter dilates or tightens, is a proto-responsiveness;
an intensity; a hubris. A blown rain with blistered sunset.
All that's civilized is pre-ordained in this excess.

Impromptus

Daylight is dragged from the windows,
calling and gesturing
from further and further off. The bird's cry
a gate closing, on the plains.

—

Butterflies uplifted
above the wet-lipped grotto,
as though uttered by a St Sebastian
skewered with the sun.

—

An old treacle-sweet tune (wrapped on a spoon
quick straps of light). Magpies must be walking about
the farmhouse lawn. And I remember how we came here under
the huge fiery litter of a wintry night.

—

Love long burning,
although ash, remains
a perfume, invincibly
in your hair, these rooms.

—

The porches of the forest are anointed with honey and blood.
In the fields, a fire rubs its hands together. Birds chime
like crystal, and flowers blanch against the lurid wall. No words
for this sky. The world is being held up in the beak of light.

—

In the vast evening, the last of daylight drifts loose
and particulate, like the sugary dust
that is blown off idly from a clear Arab sweet,
and that floats in a room's dim ultramarine.

—

There was such moonlight
that we saw him sitting late
on the hillslope, as though he were expecting
a trapdoor in the lake.

—

N.M.G.

It is you have given yourself, a child, to the care
of a stranger, after all of that talk —
you who've gone off so lightly, at a promise,
and have lain down, trusting, hand in hand with the dirt.

Small Hours

I got up early, for the lavatory,
and saw the mottled yard
that was like itself in photocopy
and the moonlight fins on cloud;

then you appeared beside me and
we held a rail as travellers might,
maybe somniloquized, touched a hand,
tried to comprehend the night;

viewed it as though a tasteful grave,
until 'Nice to meet' one of us said,
who turned towards the dark wave
of our fathomless bed.

On a Forestry Trail

A choir
of eucalyptus saplings
silvery-grey
soars
for thirty feet or more to where
their diffuse
disassembled leaf-clouds
infiltrate
the light,
and are there not so much like
insects
as harmless clouds
of commas,
or of the closing bracket-mark,
overlapping yet without
growing smudged
or dark;
those leaves are like the finely-curved scratches in
    the bark

of the saplings'
cool, stone-hard
silvery boles,
the possums' claw-marks,
now in the late afternoon's
thrown-open sky. Behind the leaves
for the moment
there is the faintest blueness,
pale
as watercolour
and yet not
delicate: it is strong with the authority
of a
deputized infinity. And in that sky,
low amongst
the at times almost organ-pipe closeness
of the trees,
there is an actual cloud, long and jutting and in the
    shape of a loaf,
but of a rich peach tone;
fresh
with the light,
this last easy left-handed gesture of the sun.
At the same time
not far off
the skull of the moon
is here, also, just the cranium,
drifting lightly,
crystalline,
and somehow it is not outdone —
these two
lying together, of an autumn afternoon.
And here, having taken hold among
a regenerated undergrowth
of bitter green —
among the serrated lantana, with its hoops like a
    barbed wire
defence — the saplings
saunter, drifting down into gullies, to the leaf-mulch
    inlay of the creeks,

and then out
onto hill-flanks
again, spreading over many acres, in a whispering
    silvery rain.
I am wandering
through tall grass, the tassel-heads
of paspalum,
along wheeltracks, not much before dark,
where the drawn-out puddles are black
as glass,
having awakened in the shape of a man,
and having a stick with which
to poke,
and an old dog,
and such rare colour
out there beside me; and all of us are
a choir.

The Life of a Chinese Poet

He was born in Tai-yuan, and lived to see the reign of six
    different emperors,
and in eighty-nine years wrote five thousand poems, in a
    rhyming prose or as songs for the *ch'in*.
It could seem that he was old from birth. His life was
    almost completely uneventful,
except for the always-remembered love that he had for a
    certain courtesan.
His mother refused to let him marry this girl, who was
    called Scented Jade,
and soon after he was ordered as a minor clerk to the far
    province of Fukien.
There he discovered, at times, the consolation of nature —
    its vividness, and its unthinkable reality.
He writes of the wild mountains, that were sharp and
    glittering as dog's teeth,
and that could be seen from amongst the hanging flowers
    of the white lanes.

The river there he also admired, which he says was like
the great dragon of Ch'i,
that turned upon itself in all the twelve directions, when
subduing the five elements.
It was his dream from youth to take arms against the
Golden Tartars,
but the northern frontiers had been made safe; there was
no fighting, but only an endless boredom there.
At fifty-four, he went home to his native village, having
never gained a preferment,
distressed by what he heard of the luxury and
incontinence of the court.
He dreamed in his work of the 'vast smoke' of chariots,
as they raced upon the plains;
he described his travels to far outposts, by night on a
river that was held within the moon's white stare.
Though he styled himself the Hermit of the Mossy
Grove, and said that he was wild, irascible and
drunken, it seems he longed for the company of
other poets.
He had married a local girl, when she was fifteen, and
spent most of his time quietly lost in his books.
Pondering both the Taoist and Ch'an Buddhist teachings,
he grew more and more enamoured of nature,
and found his companionship in mountains, flowers,
and trees.
In rainy weather he would put aside his studies and
trudge to the inn, to drink with the farming hands.
'Daily the town inn sells a thousand gallons of wine. The
people are happy: why should I alone be sad?'
He was utterly sincere in his love of beauty. The thing he
has seen appears on the white paper. There is a sense
of overbrimming life.
A Chinese critic has said, 'His poetry has the simplicity
of daily speech; in its simplicity there is depth, and in
its poignance there is tranquillity.'
When he was eighty-one, the Mongols arose once more,
and began to attack the Celestial Horde;

the armies of the Sung were continually defeated, and
were even driven out of Szechuan.
Again, he applied for enlistment, but amidst the turmoil
in the corridors at the provincial capital he was
pushed aside and ignored.
Giving up all hope that before he died he would see
himself in battle, he returned to his village in disgust.
His songs were now being sung by the muleteers in far
mountain passes, by girls bringing silk to be washed in
the streams.
In the capital, they were exclaimed over at wine parties,
and were murmured beside the Imperial Lake.
He was revered, if rarely seen, in his village, but finally
one morning the word went around that he had fallen
hopelessly ill.
Everything was made ready — the thin coffin, the two
thick quilts, and the payment for the monks;
the earth was thrown out of his grave onto the hillside,
and the incense was bought that would smoulder
among the graveposts there.
But then, the next day, he rose on his couch, and called
for wine to be brought him from the marketplace;
he had the blind rolled up on his view to the south, and
he wrote some impeccable verses, in the tonally-
regular, seven-syllable form.

Shard

One hardly thought,
seeing someone so beautiful and young,
Shall we take

the journey of indignities
together?
Now here we are,

being pressed onwards
and on,
flesh that is easily spoiled

as a pear.
But though my impulse should come
amongst the scaffolding

of Time,
if I think of you, I shall be bound
in desire again.

Going Outside

An owl is floating
in a twilight
which has the colours
of grapefruit

painted far along
behind the pines,
those ancient spears
of serrated bone.

The fluttered breast
momentarily lit.
Maybe the dog barks
because of that.

The dog's characterized
on another slope
in misty greenness
where light's draped.

And further along
the dark valley's
damp, amid the chipped
paint of trees,

a car approaches
through severed roots
of the hills, its headlights
vanishing, coming out

on a wound road.
These more bright
than the owl's place
on the after-light.

Arrivals and Departures

As late as the end of the sixties, the last part of our
        coming home
was the ten days with P&O, out from Cape Town,

in the most desolate of oceans, that has no islands
or birds or passers-by, and the waters of which are indigo,

almost black, they're so deep. That water is bulldozed by the
        wind
endlessly. And watching travellers must have known

they were climbing there a mote
in the universe, and have felt the abyss at their backs

hung open; so that often, it is said, someone leapt
into the waiting dark — the turncoat

phenomenon, of wanting to be what you most fear, taking
    its part.
And the engines' by then almost subliminal thump would stop,

as sailors attempted in some even more frail satellite
to find that person, down the shifting gullies of the sea,

amongst foliage of spray, the ship
become distant, like the day moon — that last intractable bit
    of gristle —

or an iceberg, sun-struck. And those waiting found silence was
    added
equal to the depths, as they rolled

with the rail, to watch, amid all the slide, for a head,
which had shown itself to be the darkest thing. Then they
    would go on

and come to Western Australia, often at dawn, the land
a charcoal line that was putting up light, a clear fume

from old wood; and on those always fumbling, ineffectual fin-
    gers of salty air
there'd be a smell of bush fires,

the scent of smoke from eucalyptus leaves, so clean
it must have been an exultation to some, that smell

of Australia. And then, the grandeur of their manoeuvrings at
    the dock,
that played against the voluble spray of birds, and the shine of
    rooftops,

out in a complex, living air. What fools we are
by the criteria of the senses,

of life. We want to be rid of everything difficult, and give up
    what is real;
as being rid of all that's dark, there is no light.

Illusions

That humans are a special creation, above the animals.

That the mind can exist separate from the body. (Why then would it need a body?)

That apes in outer space will find a fulfilment there.

That dreams are oracles.

That there is progress in art.

That the evil in human nature is caused by private property.

That abstracted shapes and colours make an efficient language.

That there have been works of art produced in Hollywood.

That despite their evolving with separate functions, the sexes have in all things equally matched abilities.

That the vanguard party exists in the interests of the working class.

That the Church is required as an intercessor between God and man.

That physical reality, which is always interacting, accruing minute differences, and collapsing into new forms, must be the work of a Creator.

That there is an ultimate simplicity.

That 'if God does not exist, everything is permitted.'

That there must be a God to sanction what we value as morality and beauty.

That it is not actual things we perceive, in their uniqueness and subtlety, and with such surprise, but representations of them only. (As if this distinction could mean something.)

That economics can be a science (rather than its being merely the vagaries of public morale).

That if we create enlightened laws, a bureaucracy will see justice is done.

That the greatest possible happiness and fulfilment for the species lies ahead of us. (It may lie far behind, or just behind).

That rationality is other than a rationalization of feelings.

That in a perfectly benign society, there will no longer be discontent, dissidence, and revolt.

That there is a truth apart from the pragmatic method of science.

That having denied the artist's conscious meanings and intentions, we can then appreciate the work of art (all of whose formal decisions were based on those intentions).

That this world is other than it shows itself to be.

That because 'they once laughed at the Impressionists', now everything in art that flaunts an innovatory mannerism must be good.

That post-structuralist theory is significant. (All it offers is an attitude of bad faith, and a demonstration that anything can be undermined and destroyed.)

That one should choose between the selfishness and complacency of the political right and the sentimentality and self-righteousness of the left.

That art is for art's sake. (In its sensuousness and its care, art is what Nietzsche says, 'the great stimulus to life'.)

That 'Hamlet and Lear are gay.'

That a rote iconoclasm is the way to truth. (Only that which is held above us can lift us up.)

That art requries theory. (Bad art justifies itself with theory; good art is justified by its immediate sensory appeal.)

That the microscopic is fundamental (as though it exists without the macroscopic).

That 'beauty is only in the eye of the beholder'. (Is vividness, or harmony, or gracefulness?)

That things are one, or that things are many.

That morality is spiritual. (Morality is physiology: the nervous system.)

That love is the reward for friendship. (Friendship is the reward for love.)

That the need to 'make it new' means we must overturn entirely. (Culture is continuity.)

That within the towers of the metropolis, the physical limits of our nature (which are its spiritual limits), as those evolved on the savannah, will no longer apply.

Dawn

Severing the darkness
of the wide lake, its bluish-blackness,

from a backdrop
of mountain, with which it's made one flat shape,

is a single line
of light, below the mist, that's as fine

as if surface tension
of the water, or as if within a dim garden

one saw night ebb
on the horizontal guy-line of a spiderweb.

The South Coast, While Looking for a House

Makeshift as chicken coops, houses are strewn
on
the muddy strip
of coastline, under
the escarpment's great, black
uplifted wave,
where sun goes early
off the narrow land and
the heckling pit
of the sea. This from a lofty railway
among weeds. The sun as though
an eraser is at work
in the tufted heights, reducing them
to a smear. Below,
garbage among dry stalks; newspaper, greaseproof wrap
on wire fences. A hawk balances
above a toilet block.
Of fibro
and weatherboards, houses are blowtorched

by the ocean's breath,
seem dragged
downhill on their hindquarters. In
momentary towns
around
fried chicken shops, the young, out of the surf,
are stringy, idle,
opportunistic, like nosing dogs; the old
at picnic tables, with rug and thermos flask,
shuffle
cards, the scarp
obtruding like a tumour.
The pine trees have coloured globes strung
all about them, Indians
of a travelling show.
In the afternoon, in the watery hours,
we go on, carried
toward the smoke of foundaries, of smelters, that is puffed
languidly, a pallid fungi,
on rain-coloured air.
Level crossings, iron
hammering of alarms. Then we are lifted
again, above lapsing
electricity wires, the loose
flex of coast road,
the straggling trees and
vacant ground. And the sea,
always there, slightly globed
to the swung sight, makes a context,
played off
to its startling degree. A clinical thin sheen
of afternoon,
out on the ocean, is stretched as the fitted sheet
we are handled towards.

'In one ear ...'

In one ear
when she goes out
she'll wear,

being sixteen,
a crystal
from a chandelier,

but here
her face often hangs,
hoping it's unseen,

with a more beautiful
and far
more fierce tear.

Afternoon Walk

Now the faintest sparks of rain
have touched my face and arms —
how quickly the storm comes.

It is hung like the foliage
of a wall, half along the sea,
and blows as if dust this way.

The lightning's career is like
discovering a nerve's long root.
A yacht's flame has been put out.

The liner departing, a steep dish
piled with fruit salad of light,
has disappeared in the spilt night.

I go back around the inner slope
of the headland, along a track,
narrowly amid heath and rock.

And rain, slant like sabre cuts,
strikes, as I reach the coral trees;
counters the slow sinuosities.

Leaves spin down, easily as doves,
on the bolt-heads of cobblestone.
Beyond, suburban lights coming on.

Through wet honey-coloured boles
the harbour's clay — mauve and stiff.
I find a ledge beneath the cliff.

Two lovers, in one umbrella,
have come out from somewhere near
and linger kissing, along there.

Close beside me, a taper smoke;
the one drifting woollen strand
of cobweb, afloat on the wind.

It billows, undulant as the boughs,
against all the quivering staves
that mist among architraves.

The rain's crackle and bird-notes
in leaves. Webbed light behind a frieze
of the inter-responding trees.

Leaning here, dry, rain collapses
in me. There is nothing I want back
I've ever known, or that I lack.

The Hawkesbury River

All the way out, in the wide estuary, through a cloudy
    morning light,
to the Caledonian-seeming mountains
that are black
in the sea, the waters are moving shortly upon themselves
with their insect-leg movements — a sawing, gently,
gently.
The entire water
is a slinkily-moving milky silver.

While closer, beneath these high, forest-blackened promonto-
    ries,
drawn to our left, darkly
as drapes,
are dissolutions of the bank,
big cell-divisions —
the river, in this part, going through its cold repertoire
of Munch-like shapes.

There is hardly a breeze, and we're alone. I can imagine us,
seen from one of the few shacks
embedded here and there
in the eucalyptus slopes, with the curled shape of the jib
borne on this fullness, at the pace
of a leaf, that as yet
is well before the weir.

We left, impelled by first light, from mud-banks in their smoke,
were carried off
like smoke, and reached this empty runway
while it was still reverberant
with the sun,
although utterly quiet.
The only notable sound was the lightly-bounced water
making an applause
beneath our gently tupping

sloop, on finding
it is wood.

Now, through the short day, we two are leaning back into our
    bodies;
and we cut ourselves bread,
cheese, and fruit,
and pour wine, and watch the broad pelicans alight
on skidding feet,
with their wings of a sudden held up
in cavernous shape,
before they fold neatly as Swiss army knives,
and we idly talk,
in moving back and forth about this wide place, although alert
to every slightest
breeze.

Sometimes, rarely today,
under the steep, rounded hills, that are set deep
in the lake-like water,
with its glass bottle dark —
these hills made up entirely of tight replicas
of their own shape, except where,
in a bowed facade,
there are the occasional sunlit
columns —
sometimes today, below these hills, there has been another yacht;
such purity of form
only matched
by Brancusi's 'Bird in Flight'.

Among the headlands we keep passing, one that we have taken
    for our mark
is a blocked-out sphinx shape —
against its dark flank
single birds

glide, at times, remote as satellites,
blinking and white. Until now, behind one of those, you
    become aware
the hills are resuming
an older mood.
You see how there is coming upon this place something
more basic (a circling back
within limitation), which is like an encounter with the locked metal
underneath our clothes
and skin.

And as we think of turning home, in the as-yet mild winter
    afternoon,
the sail flaps
and the wind runs down.
But the long-whiskered sun keeps stalking on, or it is bowled
away like a beach grass, sea-urchin shaped;
it lurches behind the cowls
of the cloaked landscape.

At once, miasmas start to return, floating across the figured dark.
The blocky rubble along the shoreline has already sunk
into night.
The water, where it was for a time striped finely with moving
    silver,
and interspersed with dots,
complex and fast,
has been erased.
Lying still propped on the hatch-top, I have grown chill,
in all this stretched-apart
downward access
of the dark.
And with nothing that can be done,
I recall,
of a sudden, how my bare wet feet were brushed, back there,
wound, dried,
for a moment — as though in an old dream,

an old
absurdity — with some of the hair
of the sun.

Through a high valley
which is slowly turning around
upon us, that hoves above, blackly, there appears a broken
        orange yolk,
in coarse strings
across the lesser dark. And the water flaps,
flaps, but can barely move us on — its sound melancholy
        and hollow
as the dry-blown notes
of an Andean flute.
Though almost becalmed, we are coming athwart
a thin lane
of lit water, that down all of its drawn-out length
is made of little incipient spurts
of light — these
ineffectual, as the motor that is failing
and failing
to ignite.

I have come to stand around now at the bow, so that I can
        watch dwindle,
so I can see
solemnly recede
into the mountain, from where I lean out in the rigging,
what could be
that pale long procession of butter lamps.

Lineations

The Sideboard

A car passes at the corner,
the damp street grown silvery and still.
Two of the curtains saunter
beside a shadowy window sill —

the living room, silent as yet,
at my aunts'. As though it's the Ark
of the Covenant, they've set
each treasure, in the semi-dark,

on a sideboard: girls with piper
in a soap-white nude porcelain;
photographs framed in twined silver;
lacquer bowls; a blond manikin;

a butterfly of opal; a plaster
Madonna with plastic tear.
Quietly, as if a cat burglar,
I find out their lost selves in here.

The aunts, one genteel but drunken,
one with only a rat-trap thrill
livening her eyes, have forgotten
about me — gone over the hill

and far away; and I sit on
with old books' caramelised gleam,
light in a tortoise-shell fan,
prickled glass, the cloud's purple dream.

Ritual

At times a cloud, when you have paused deep in the
    mountains,
throws its shadow on the upland grass, and this darkness
brought early into the world is like a ferryboat grounding,
that carries a warrior you must confront.
The red gout of a leaf drips from a nearby twig
as though it were flung there. Cicadas are crying
the truth about our lives, with their armour discarded
on dead leaves. Now await you only the long regrets
of the night camp, where your life seems already over
and its sins all that are yours. You grasp, for a moment,
at lines trailing after the birds through the twilight sky
and step forward, into a suddenly steaming void,
as the cloud lifts its hatches. Yellow slopes are swirling.
Right foot and then left foot. Why hesitate, and why grieve?
For you've attained nothing, and so can lose nothing,
not since beginningless time. You have never yet seen
the face of this antagonist, because of a sudden
you strike, with all force, from out of yourself, and are cut
by only a breeze of night. Yet, you hardly can doubt
suave hair was bound quickly in a knot and slung across
a shoulder, and sleeves fell, as those heavy forearms rose.

A Traveller

The blunt engine of the sleeping-car train
appears, carriages black,
while it takes a long curve, its headlight's stain
through ferns beside the track.

And wavering along tight poles of eucalypts,
across their vanished height,
making them seem stage curtains, with deep pleats
in grey, the bare spotlight.

The Circus

An old and unregenerate world
is overnight unfurled
on the park — something from the fifties
and from the medieval centuries;
it has changed less than the Church
and comes to smutch
a wealthy reserve, beside the yacht club and tennis court.
I'm walking late
when the circus arrives here, through our liberals'
      confusion.
It's without flambeaux: the power generation
is on a truck. Those spatulate shadows, in the foggy night,
unload at the point, in blue light.
A ring-in myself, I have to go
around there, on the empty harbour-front walk; and I see
      someone throw,
at once, a huge grey tongue,
with other offal, upon the grass — it dangles its string
as if a bouquet
that's been ordered for a Salomé.
The caravans are parking anywhere, with their backs to
      the harbour,
now after midnight, and hunger
makes the tiger shout
in the shadows, pacing out
four strides, and then back — dreadful to watch
the rapid tension of this match,
so dripping and furious.
Someone comes staggering towards it already, solicitous
with a sloppy tub
full of snake-tunnelled hearts and of watery blood.
Car lights, behind a dark colonnade
of great Moreton Bay fig trees, back by the road,
appear and disappear, like coins dropped
into a pool, where the water's slopped

and clears, rapidly and intermittently — those people
    drifting unaware
of the forthrightness here.
I'm back soon after dawn,
and the workers are out already, also unshaven.
True, at this hour, that the creases
in the men's looks make furtive and bitter places.
They've teeth missing, and they smoke and spit,
and are ravaged or overweight.
People have lined up with buckets at a tap
and portable toilets are set up
beyond the laid-out small tents. I'm surprised to see
a huddle of dwarfs. One comes straight across to me,
    truculently,
glares out of his squashed shape,
the legs buckled, and with his hair in a 'flat top',
and tells me to piss off; then he strides
back, ignoring the duckboards.
His brow is pressed into a deep crease, beneath
    its curlicue,
and his wide-splayed legs,
from behind him, are worked like an African canoe,
where one digs
either side, heavily, to row.
Such curiosity of mine is thoughtless, I know.
A foetid smell of steamy green piss
and of soaked straw and dung hangs over all this.
I walk toward the morse code, jubilant water.
Here they have sat, wrapped up, sinking toward
    his centre,
nodding, one of their old men.
Life shows this kindness to some, in getting them
    ready for oblivion.
The harbour's all the stardust and spangles
around here, but hard to ignore the circus, as it steps
    from its tangles,
the tent rising like a gown. I cross to the elephants,
    having seen

two accidentally bump and begin a routine,
a soft shoe, in slow motion,
swaying weightlessly, like plants underneath the ocean.
Then each is once more inert,
as though dangled from a crane. They'll scuff the padded foot
occasionally, and scatter chaff
in a throw-away gesture, that is like a hollow laugh.
Every inch of them is cross-scored and dried
as palings, weathered
among the sand dunes. They're clothed in tarpaulins,
loose-fitting as tendons
of an old man's throat. Skinny girls have come out,
    whose skin
is almost neon white. One hangs a lurid washing, and
    they lean
on guy-ropes, a moment, in the sun.
(A baby that's tripped in the mud is a nuisance and
    no-one's armful.)
They're dressed for rehearsal
in scanty fishnet tights, drawn high on their loins,
and are loose yet sinewed. Paltry as coins,
it might seem, but they have the discipline of their artistry,
as well as whatever cliché
they share with us, of longing and hurt.
The big cats are driven out
of their cages, into the tent — the carts drawn up like a tail,
and the animals, goaded on, trail
well apart, from door to open door, then down a wire
    tunnel,
crouching, as into a funnel,
so that they burst forth, surging upwards impressively
within. The tiger's last, and runs the cages' full length
    directly,
low-slung, swift as a train engine
when unencumbered, treading each piston.
It can move fast as a wasp does in attack.
One hears a whip or pistol crack
inside. The male lion, with big grassy head-dress and
    shrunken stem,

went with heavy clearing of phlegm;
meditative, resentful. An emblematic flower,
wilting. It is toothless, no doubt, but like Baudelaire's
    the rancour
of the sideways looks,
to remind us about the rumour of a swordstick, of its
    gloveful of hooks.
Leaving, I see the old man
is dozing on. Set for a lookout, this graduand
has nothing to tell us. Except, to make us hope that
    we perform
as calmly, in the face of final harm.
I look back and there is an elephant
being hosed, that's lambent;
and I wait a few minutes, to see if it wears for a hat
the morning's first crisp yacht.

'Out rowing ...'

Out rowing at night
on the river

voices

in the stillness
some cabins

among

the shoreline
in one

a bottle is opened

any of those might be
a lantern

that I could hold

Nambucca Heads

Shaped like a 'lady's finger',
a biscuit-coloured sandbar;
the estuary is blue china.

Behind the dunes are swamp oak;
amongst them, a tin-roof shack
with a rolled sail of beige smoke.

The nearest navy-blue mountain
is fluted like a blown curtain.
On summer afternoons the rain

slops, big as white grapes each drop,
for an hour. A rowboat drawn up
by the shack's tomato crop,

and the collapsing fence is
under passionfruit vines like sheaves.
Amid the cabbages, rain seethes.

A fig tree above the river,
the inland side, will grow circular
at dusk. There, cattle wander

the flat bronze paddocks. Tall poles
in haze, to the smoke-blue hills.
By the coast, eucalyptus-shoals —

this foliage is like dolphins;
rolling shapes, and leaping ones
in places. Close-packed, it shines

with a salt spray of light. Strung
from headlands, the beaches are long
bows — glisten of vibrant string.

Out on the river's great billow
comes the train, that is trundled slow
on metal trestles, with below,

more loosely, the white pelicans.
Leaning in his shack, an old man's
waved. Then, as each iron roof shines,

a slant, strewn town's revealed. Whether
dawn or dusk, it chimes silver,
as in tall rain. Here the river,

on humid-fleshed nights, sways sequins;
ophidian-dark. And neon's
red mist, on the veal-pink dawns.

Still this flaked ocean, blazing like
a furnace, after a night's work,
breathes mildness. O white Pacific.

Über Deutschland

Outside the tall hotel's
windows, of a sudden,
appears an unwinding
belated snow, the big

shreds loosely-fleshed, tatty.
These guttural, thickly-
uttered, wet syllables
of a stumbling snow. All

of it suggesting the
bitterest outcome for
a letter, that is cast
out, exploded. We're at

the beginning of spring
and here's a redundant
and long over-ripe snow.
But in the dim cinema

of our room, it is we
are carried down, sinking
steadily, in a long
pan, we who seem settling

directly, as in a goods
lift, through such various
up-draughts, lateral drifts,
vortices, and flurries.

The thick veil of 'atoms
in the void' slackens now
briefly and secretly
and shows within itself

one floating edifice —
beer hall or hunting lodge.
We go out, to dispel,
perhaps, the sinking; to

snow that is put out as
embers are at night, in
touching us. And find a
bit of jollity, a bit

of quick-stepping, as beer-
bellies remove, mincing
and raucous, indoors. The
Germans are like the Church

and being nice, these days.
Over cake shop, laundromat,
there arises, fascistic,
iron-black, and bristling, a

cathedral — silhouette
of the Gothic forest.
About its spires, along
the alley of building-tops,

furiously, the low clouds
are carried on, unrelieved:
racing and entwining like
cords of an icy, slush-

thickened water; undulant,
spilling, hurtling towards
circumstance. These whirling
wings of the locust horde.

Version

With my face pressed all day against the glass
we crossed a distant plain;
I watched how the steppes were heavily drawn past
from the smoky train.

And saw clouds and rivers slipping away, too,
hills fold and unfold.
Adrift on the earth, what is it that keeps you?
What is it we can hold?

In the glass, I watched her face that mornings made
glow amber as honey,
and noon simmered olive oil in colonnades
among pines' greenery.

Paused at night, heard a fog horn on the harbour
as a ship left the earth.
This when I'd forgotten not to remember.
I would have liked a berth.

All one has might as well be water dangling
where birds light upon
the boughs — of a sudden, there has come a wing
and it's shattered and gone.

What we are is this pressure, that's not our own;
unrelieved, redeployed.
It will pulse and congeal in the dark again
when all worlds are destroyed.

A Pine Forest

In autumn windows, evening's land
of ebony and fire. Out there stand
the pines, shingled on the valley;
and cold rises off them early,
exhaled across the axe-carved hills.
Above this now, a liquor swirls
in the clear glass of dusk, that's lit
already with a small starlight
for highlights — the fiery water
is brandished, reflects a grandeur
beyond here, or a roaring wassail,
most likely, chaotic, brutal.
These pines that I gaze on arouse
disquiet in me. In early hours,
while staying here, I walk among them,
every day in a damp chasm,
a gloom. Insurgent in this country,
they're alien. 'The Ghost of a Flea',
Blake's drawing of his monstrous vision,
comes to mind. On television
one saw the origin of this trope —
they showed within a microscope
demonic fleas, and other mites.
The quiet trees recall such parasites
for me. (And are, in their tight band,
too dark, too military, in a land

that naturally wears the various,
airy, open eucalyptus —
those more casual, improvised things;
each floating its kites, on many strings.)
Under the pines, heavy needles
seem insect droppings and dead cells
coating a nest; the spiked antlers
and broken teeth, struggling creatures'
armoury; and the plated boles,
bristling, moss-infected, are scales.
Such life pronounces too gloweringly
that it's survival machinery.
Seen afar, sluggish in midday smoke,
the history that the trees evoke,
matted, and drawn into a mass,
is horrible, insalubrious.
(I think of great war paintings by Dix
that one can't love, but one respects.)
The light is a fire, just too far
away for harm, set where we are.

9 Poems

I sit and watch
the way that rain is falling,
its eyes closed.

As if one dead
had laid an arm around
your shoulders, wintry sun.

After a quarrel
she makes love in the shower
to the limbs of water.

A shell thrown out
by the ocean drives onwards
to infinity.

The crows go over
all day, back and forth, anxious
to lace night with night.

Writing beneath vines;
a Sunday. The slow, clean strokes
of the cricket match.

Bring my mother in
from the morning, she will vanish
in that light.

The shadowy sides
of everything, on the way down
to the white sea.

In the vase, flowers
from deep in the heathland
open their eyes.

Acceptance Speech

Stopping in the tangle
of a garden, in the early morning, amongst its frettings,
dangles,
and overlays, I have disappeared
for a moment, in a fragrance.

It was as if it were the light which knew the light
on the overwhelmed grass;
as though
it were itself that smelled the dampness
in this perfume.

The damp air, which came thinly from off the dead leaves
and the reeds,
Hermes.
As when a breast is turned in the hand, some further
    minute degree,
a mouth opens, the pure waters fall.

Such an acceptance, as in that moment, accepts all that is
as indivisible; sees it is dependent
on everything in time.
It is this which you did not understand
in all your other lives.

Passage

The train is long and slow
and curves away
as though
one saw upon a leaf
the detour of a worm

it is dragging between
the lilies
white

and flagrant
outside the bedroom

each bloom
in the green light
is filled with rain
a syrup
in a tall stirrup cup

and the mosquito it would seem
this bit of soul
this little grey appetite
would like to stamp
its fibrils

upon the air
the way that it keeps pacing
tightly and frustrated
wavering and drawn
tracing

a freely-treated shape
it wants
hovering something of that drink
while the train
that rattled the stony panes

near sundown
and the sunlight drawn straight
a wet blond
across the forest top
are gone

in the time that it has taken
for the windows to be shut.

Coastline

A burned caramel sky to westward
for a sunset
above the lights of the towns
in a thin rain.

The thistle-tops of the headlights
are refrigerator blue,
along a curving highway, under
the broken range.

An ocean, that wears grey gauze,
collapses like a lung
upon the beach. A black dog is searching
by the sad wall.

Beneath dark shelves of the pine trees,
deep in the wetness
of a garden, there are white curtains
that might be columns.

Aisles and arcades, all deserted, except
for people with rags
tied about them. The flame lit here to some effect
is above the refinery.

And neon keeps on with its performance
as wearily
as a cocktail waitress. We climb from the town
into a washed twilight.

The star that is now wriggling there
like a crook'd finger
has a maliciousness, it would seem,
that is very old.

Impromptus

Moonlit night; the willows
have drawn their curtains. A calm
on the face of the main street. A shadow
takes a shadow's hand.

A moth at nightfall grabs the porch light
like a man drowning on a slippery buoy. Shutters clash,
sand trickles out of the wall. A lemon tree has inclined
to the long curlicued whisperings of the dust.

In the new suburbs, in light rain,
at the road's verge treading its line
with the stateliness of a tightrope walker,
it might seem, the diesel roller.

On wet sand, a dog goes trotting, way ahead;
the spume is blown across his plume.
He doesn't look back, and so neither do I,
and we will be quenched in the dark.

Under a cliff, stones
in sea-mist, and a stag's bones
caging a butterfly, hung
blackly as blood and fluttering.

Still with my head lowered
at the desk, I hear
the stream again.
Is it golden now, or violet?

To find a room within the waves,
a lamp of honey, beneath the salt. . . .
The wet lianas are ascending
through the lightning, at night.

A Garage

In one of the side streets
of a small hot town
off the highway

I noticed the garage,
its white boards peeling
among the grey paling fences.

There was a lone petrol pump,
from the sixties, perhaps,
out in the sun-blaze.

With its human scale
and humanoid appearance
this had a presence —

it seemed the man-servant
of our adventures on the road,
the doorman of our chances.

We pulled in, for nostalgia,
onto concrete. From where
did this thing's subtle

almost avoidable sense
of sacrifice and remorse
arise? One could feel it

as though it were a line held
in the hand, drifted far out
somewhere, unweighted.

Who was this, in weathered
blue outfit, with badge,
expressionless small head,

and rubbery arm across
to its shoulder, either dutifully
or out of diffidence?

Was it presenting arms, and in
servitude or willingness?
Such stoicism discomforts,

implies a threat, and rebellion.
Elusive as music, our feelings
are blown through us. How

to interpret them? — Some person
dependable but dangerous,
solicitous and sinister. I looked off

down a blank street, of pines,
telegraph poles, old houses
in deep yards, that made

a genuflection, in approaching
gentian hills. And then into
the garage, a long dark

barn, an empty corridor
in the galaxy, with somewhere
far along it one star

crackling and flaring
bluely. And then at the black
dog, in its narrow shade.

And at the old bowser —
a feeling still proclaimed and
ungraspable, in the light.

Someone had shouted
acknowledgement, and so we sat
quietly there. The light

had become an interest
of this place, pronounced
by contrast with the peculiar

matt blackness of sump-oil
stains, widely soaked
into earth, gravel, and cement.

A blackness that was opaque
as the diversions
of the tunnelling heart.

His Muse, to Dylan Thomas

'If I were tickled by the rub of love ...',
if I was tickled by the rubber glove,
excuse me, doctor. That was not love.

Flight at Dusk

At eighteen thousand feet we have come
into the presence of a storm
that is purplish-black. Like an oak, and then pine,
this flared shape. The vast trunk is rain.
Yggdrasil, with roots in Hell,
its boughs through Heaven, in reversal —
Hell is a synonym of falling,
ventured on here; the rain is blessing
the ground. Far beneath, dustily,
what had seemed a landscape seen indistinctly
is only cloud. Streaming cobwebs.
All over this tree, lightning stabs;
a twitching, darting — it's the constant strife
and nerves of insect and bird life.
Unlike Satan, we are coasting
the walls of Darkness. On our western wing
we lean, too, and despondently
we sink. — A mosquito, so minutely.
The wind has shifted: there is no chance to run
from such nuclear explosion —
as though stepping on ice, our small craft
lurches, dithers, in just the draught.
(At dusk, the owl of Minerva's flight
has begun, that brings us insight.)
I turn to incomplete work
spread on my lap. When next I look
the moon I had seen, a fine bowl dripping
one star, where it tilted, is vanishing,
and the stripe of ultramarine, lit
like an ad for a Turkish sweet.
I feel, though I keep on working here carefully,
disgust. So passive, so arbitrary.

Note

It has always seemed to me that natural things would help us
if only we could hear
the eloquence
of their dumb ministry.

What is it that these things of the world do?
They submit,
and they endure.
They flourish. They don't ask for anything.

They simply take what is given.
They flourish,
all at once, where it had seemed they were merely enduring.
Everything can touch them.

We are searching for the world, amongst this diversity
of existence,
that has formed itself so loosely
in a ramshackle system.

While our lives, one can see, are just a routine sacrifice,
consumed and forgotten,
off somewhere to one corner
in the courts of the sun.

What can last? Only what we have made
and hand on
amongst ourselves, that is withering in our hands,
but never known without us.

So we take the dark roads
in beautiful clothing, greeting each other;
sorry for the void
that cannot see what we've become.

A Sight of Proteus

For Ted and Kathy Hillyer

These squat or long-drawn shapes, like toadstool caps,
are sandstone rocks
in silhouette, against a silvery band of ocean
of an afternoon,

as I climb down from the track along the cliff-tops
and pause, on opportunistic steps,
above gravel
in the shingle pits,

that lie below those ramparts on the wide rock tables;
where you can walk
at eye-level
with the running-in of the surf. I look back

along the cliff-face, its facets
grey and fissured
as a Picasso, cubist period,
and see how the bushfire-swift, white surfline ignites

and drives smoke
toward shore, while the sea out from here is a deep navy,
past where the sun props
one arm behind it, and is calm and empty.

Below, the waves dragging off the black rock platform
are a stark root-system,
or a backward-sucked lightning screen,
pronged, a few moments, in relative slow-motion.

Awaiting me, obliquely, is a deserted beach, and those wisps
of she-oak, that complain
delicately, it seems, behind it; and on the low dunes
are beach vines

and the aqua-coloured grass, that leans
onto any breeze,
as compliant as shadows.
The light in the wet shore has a metallic sheen

as if great ventilator shafts
are sunken there. And one can see — braced on the rocks of this
    corner,
in hope of dolphins —
how the river flatly drifts

parallel with the dunes, and has sand
banked shining within it, and how the mangrove island
is all white birds,
settled there like the chips of light on part of the water.

This river as slowly as possible comes around
to its estuary. The town,
under the headland's smooth grass haunch and the reservoir,
is the poles for light and telephone,

a block of wooden flats (which I know says Vacancy),
the steep roofs of pub and general store,
a cross, the signs on the hamburger and video joints, and the fibro
or timber houses, climbing from their hollow

with the climbing bitumen,
onto a cleared and scrubby hillside.
The mountains, far beyond, are drawn to left and right,
and their flat facade

is transient
as convolvulus, in colour,
and this affects their form, and their locality,
or it does seemingly.

Earlier, when setting out,
I saw a girl from town run down the shore,
passing her clothes to a friend, and, coiling up her black hair
one-handed, at the last moment,

dive beneath a wave. She swam
easily to where some boardriders had settled in the sun,
then lay back among them,
talking, tilted in the sea that passed,

her body white through the clear surface of those rollers,
the bikini-bottom like a shadow;
and only now
she returns, with the other kids, striding back strongly
        onto shore.

Sometimes the fishermen work from down there,
using a great net
immemorial style: wading out, while two undo it from a
        rowing boat
that is the last of its floats,

and they take the catch right at their front door.
They draw
a broad welcoming one-armed embrace upon the water
that turns crushing.

I saw them do this toward evening, as the few boardriders
        came home,
who rode above the net-hem,
hot-dogging and stylish; and the men, hanging on,
shouted at them,

calling someone a young bastard;
one probably his father.
Some women, sometimes, and other men
from the pub, each of those holding a glass or beer can,

come and sit in the dunes,
but not much chiacking goes on, as the surf totters
the older workers, thigh-deep, who take the strain, and cuffs
    the others
in their faces.

They know when a school of fish is about to pass this town
by a fire a lookout will set
a match to, on top of the headland
beneath which I stand. That sight

brings them running from the pub,
while others drive, and hauling their net from a trailer,
carrying it in file —
it is dark as the seaweed along the shore, in its roll.

And when they pick
the fish they want, there on the beach, they pack
these in plastic
and ice, and onto the four-wheel drives, backed up;

which, to an aesthete watching,
is a pity, particularly
the carving-up of the shore; and then they race back
to a cold-room shed, near the railway.

With twilight, the long prow of tumbled-down rock
before this headland
is surrounded by an almost luminescent
foam, constantly elastic;

and a loose breast-pocket handkerchief of whiteness
appears, against black stone,
from time to time, with a notable flourish, and is being
    re-tucked
as you look again.

Out to sea, the water's become
a rich greenish-grey, oil-streaked it would seem
with violet, and the sky
a dark violet-grey.

And there is something extraordinary sailing by —
an arctic cloud,
shelved and squared, and upreared out of the horizon,
lit from far inland, where the sun has almost disappeared;

blue, apricot and rose veils shifting within its white.
Though, such a sight
fades very soon: the power turned off, it loses splendour
    and form
as you watch.

And now the low black mountain rim
is gilt-fringed
far along, with a light that has been hived here, progressively,
in the surf, and sealed away.

There's a last surfrider, just there,
and another one, moving from beyond some rocks;
each in the mild air still waiting astride
his board,

although it's invisible, from where I look down.
They seem, in drifting clear
of the shadows, to be giants, who are standing out
amid the sea's tremor, those myriad oil-cups of low blue light.

The closest one, an old hippie, is bald, with a flag-like beard
and a carved build, and he folds his arms
like a Greek sea-god,
who looks in across that blowing hem

to the flimsy town. No longer hidden,
he is considering going ashore, or he longs to, and living in
    this place
so 'backward' and 'slow',
where the smoky streetlights have come on.

Isolate Evenings

The Japanese ink, moist on the stone —
stroking a moonlit pelt,
or it is blackest wine.

A subtle carbon perfume to this tablet
being worked. It is a joyful
accumulation, towards sleep.

Beach Shack

It's wisteria-grown, but I
push back the gritty, cracked window,
just arrived. The usual storm,
soon. Grass looks withered, even so.

A slanted fence, where magpies fall.
The east is tar, paint-slapped thickly,
and the scalloped surf keeps passing
along the heads, radiantly.

At most times drab, now the other
white places on this slope throw back
a light that's granular, over-proof.
Broken pickets, then water's black,

on which the foam rises and soars
to land, ablaze in its spread flight.
About the yard amble warbling
those magpies, closed in black and white.

Philip Hodgins (1959-1995)

Your funeral recalled for me your poems;
I seemed to feel your touch about it all —
sparse trees nearby, sinuous, stringy gums,
their leaves, rags on barbed wire; the lustrous call
of furious magpies; clay instead of tombs;
and low weather, with dry weeds and thistle
that we came wandering over, scatteredly,
to the coffin, strung above its cavity.

The empty place the world is hung upon.
'No speeches, only verse,' in your dicta.
I read one of those pieces you had chosen,
'Sailing To Byzantium'. How bitter
the humour, the irony, you'd added. Then,
because there'd dried up here part of the delta
of the Murray, it seemed right that Les spoke —
spontaneously brilliant, a common bloke.

Hartley and Paul read briefly. That was all.
Backyards of wooden houses, fairly near.
Each of us threw into the eight-foot hole
a flower. But first, had to stand and hear
ropes slowly creak, unwound from a steel rail —
a labour to breathe, stopping; heads bowed there.
At a mullock heap, along that gravel track,
out in Victoria, something gold put back.

Just nights before your twelve-year fight was up
you rang. 'Tell them I was a great hater,'
you said. The Literature Board's lucky-dip,
demoralising to a true writer;
feminists' self-pitying career; French slop,
that only 'signs' exist (hearts of water);
treasonous clerks in the university ...
condemning these you'd call your best elegy.

You were as loyal as a classic Roman;
vehement and pure; a believer in style;

stoic, yet glamorous like Wilfred Owen;
the exemplar of an Australian school —
going straight for the pay-dirt of emotion,
laconic, pragmatic and sceptical.
'Live another thirty years!' If I do,
it'll seem a moment, then. I'll think of you.

The Sea-Wall

The headland has been raided,
eaten, broken away —
a carcass that hyenas
have found. It is the quarry

for the wall, this drawn-forth
rough intestine of stone;
a tight jumble of shapes like
DNA or protein.

Among these, a concrete path
goes nowhere, to carry
with bold gesture to sea
just tracks of the railway

that built it (now rust flakes
and the sleeper's imprint).
Tipped each side, more recent,
are huge blocks of cement.

What purpose the wall served
has been lost (apart from
that of swimmers and paddlers).
Now, no ships ever come.

On the wall, looking back past
broken edge and sharp angle,
the line of the headland
holds this concrete and shale

beneath an undulant
stroke of grass, like green fur,
against blue panes of stone.
The air, a mode of fire.

I've seen the wall at dawn
from that grass: in silhouette,
a stamen weighed with seed,
on the sea's milky-white.

People come there early
and sit on flat roof-tops
of their small, skewed pueblo
that they drape with bright stripes.

And here they weed the garden
of the sea, in alcoves,
or snorkel above rocks,
and laugh when ocean shoves

heavily — a whale, with spume —
the outside curve. They cover
just eyes and genitals,
organs of too much pleasure.

About them, soap flakes sprinkled,
then higher on the sea
soap powder, then lathered clouds,
or the whole crisp laundry.

Children come cycling by,
and men scrape fish they've caught;
a woman's on the ocean
with a red towel drawn straight

behind her, which she levers
slowly back and forth; her breasts
solemnly eye those passing;
the finest sea-spray floats

in hair on forearms, on
a girl's lip; feet are slapped
through puddles; in long chevrons
of shade, picnics unpacked.

The sea's striped purple, blue-green
and chrome. An idle yacht;
a black dog against its shape,
on a pedestal, alert.

Slightly-curved, like fishing rods,
this wall unfailingly
sprouts its riffled sparse hairs,
especially on Sunday.

To John Olsen

On your workbench were scattered some goose quills,
beside broken charcoal, inky bottles,
one unused. This, a sill of twig-brushed snow,
or smoothly threaded white sand, when the flow
of ocean's edge has left a glaze revealed.
With licked fringe, all fibres perfectly sealed,
buoyant and raked, resting at quiff and horn,
this line, as you noticed, had your guest drawn.
You trimmed its tip, to demonstrate for me
the calligraphic possibility
in such an implement. Not when it flew
was it more supplely used; and it grew
in stature, out of your fist. The winged grip
put wings to your mind — every surge, each dip,
of mountains, ranging far off, were caressed
by your gaze, ink proved, their space possessed.
I tried it. Perfect balance in the hand;
the hollow spine weighed by the air it fanned.
This not designed, except through increments
of spontaneous change, by accidents,
that breed, when used opportunistically.
I thought, too, Red Indians' dignity

was conferred upon them by the eagle
feathers they gathered — how not be regal
and alert, underneath those crowns they wore.
I glimpsed this, while you urged me on to draw;
and dipping with that heroic billow,
traced the bleached draperies outside Lithgow.
'Look at that,' you cried, and presented me
the instrument for such discovery.
I wanted then to continue to ply
this great quill, felt imperious as Bligh,
possessed by a sagacity like Cook's,
but there was more to learn — turned to your works,
and found amongst them their diversity.
I admired a more languid quality
in your brushwork; so Aboriginal,
its ease, its slowness; this the very style
of our impassive land: like campfire smoke,
eucalypt boughs, shorelines, creeks. You evoke
a Chinese spirit, too — the passive strengths,
so awesome, of earth and water. Those great lengths
your lines sustain are time, then timelessness.
How Taoist, the reins you give to looseness,
and tauten, just where you need. You've the skills
that suit this place. Your marks become tendrils
of waterlilies, inky waterholes,
the fur of caterpillars, the great boles,
slowly surging, of gum trees, scribbled knots
of foliage, speckled pond-life, mallee roots.
These trails, watery or tarred, are aerial
(native again): concepts, yet sensual.
Starting with *art brut*, the fashion once, you
acclimatised it — had this land strike through.
Your project's to 'write the landscape' for us,
newcomers and homeless; and a chorus
in your talk is, 'Drawing is empathy.'
This was at lunch, with wine deployed freely
for all but strong Michael, who was driver.
Outdoors, under crumbling wisteria,
crumbling our bread; the peacock's display
stalking this. Formerly a seminary,

your place's casements open on the foam
of acres of roses; on pine groves; a dome
of hill above, doodled with scrub, a line
of jet's vapour angled behind. The wine
encouraged my playful provocation,
that drawing's design. 'It's superstition,'
you said, 'sympathetic magic — the edge
Picasso had.' We accept the adage
it's based in accidents. Your mind's pliant
as your line: our elder, you're complainant
against all rigidities, including
the modernistic — cubist fracturing
you much deride. 'Every emphasis
in art means loss. Who can talk of progress?'
On our way home, I drooped in the back seat ,
all windows down, struck by long shafts of heat.
Through the Blue Mountains, in raiding traffic;
less *art nouveau* forest, each year more brick.
Your feather lay lightly as a Nile boat
beside me — next thing, I saw it afloat
upon a flood tide; lifted by the draught
a stampeding truck had made. 'Plucked,' I laughed
ruefully, 'the last time.' That truck was gone,
its wheels revolving like sawmill blades, on
down the highway, in free fall, with my quill
riding the slipstream, a windsurfer's sail.
On gilt-shot air, blue smoke-burst eucalypts,
the feather's cursiveness; its catch at slips;
a rapier exploring; arabesques
above traffic behind (we loved those risks);
then, flung to the bush, defiant ensign.
I thought, 'I wish John could have seen that line.'

Wintry Dusk, Bellingen

From orange grass sticks a boneyard of trees,
the night seated early under these hills,
and fibrous bushes twitch on wires of breeze —
theatrical brown flames. Evening distills
its ether, dark tree-line for sediment.
The sight of a dam's blind cataract chills.
On a last slope, the sun's emollient.

The forest's dim facade is whitely clawed.
Isolate trees step forth, wanting to speak.
Below, heavily-laddered, a dirt road;
above, aluminium, and birds stroke,
quivering like wind-pressured drops of sleet
along a screen. Quickly congealing, smoke
from a broken pillar that's red as meat.

At dusk, cellophane dimness of the world.
Two white cockatoos are raucous, over
the moon's ulcerous face, that's now revealed.
A paddock curves like a falling river,
and down through deep grass the dark fence posts ride.
Pointing everywhere, the dead trees gesture
as if they'd been in panic when they died.

Epigrams

So this is the castle
of your ideals —
now show me the dungeon.

Landscape painters are the priests
and missionaries, and their art the sacrament,
of my religion.

Good is the conclusion
we draw from evil. We call good those things
that could benefit us.

Poetry is made of words, Mallarmé claimed,
which is not exact —
feelings exist as images, not as words.
(Images are the language in which we dream.)

Those who devalue pleasure
for themselves are most likely to undervalue
pain for others.

A style in art is an attitude
to experience. Looked at this way, a style can seem
ridiculous (e.g. Mondrian's).

Moral pleasure is reassurance
about the nature of human beings —
This is what we find so moving
in a work of art.

The great mystery of nature
is that it should be nothing but itself.
One has the sense of something supreme
in the most ordinary of things. . . .

The senses can mislead us,
it is true — when we rely upon
only one of them.

What one loves about nature
is its unresponsiveness —
it is, precisely,
that it 'neither cares nor knows'.

The sensory pleasures of the world
are not merely transitory —
a denigration the otherworldly have made —
but can be seen as constantly
renewed and refreshed for us.

All aesthetic judgements
are self-evident. Since they are comparative,
one need only point.

What we consider good in others
is their altruism, which we praise out of selfishness.
If we practise unselfishness ourselves,
it is for a selfish motive —
for accolade (not the least our own).

We feel nature act in us, and think
we originated the impulse,
but all of our identification
comes after the event.

Reply to Nietzsche: It is not possible
to live amongst other people
and to create one's own values.

We are all Protestants now:
all individualists
to a once-inconceivable degree.

The world, it seems, is the maximum
number of things, or of forces,
that can exist together.

Épater les bourgeois? Certainly,
but there is another complacency one mustn't
overlook. *Épater les avant-gardistes.*

Sapientia Lachrimarum

The sound of the heat's the cicadas' note —
a drilling that forces sweat to the brow.
Or coloratura of the earth's throat

vibrates in the clearing, while eucalypts grow
silvery shafts — these pistons with their steam
about them. And neither can you follow

this intensity, and throng — there's no beam,
no mote, that's undissolved in the light's stare.
The forest ascends with a smoothness and gleam

that is oiled. It seems you're caught by a flare,
stepping into day. Withdrawn to a shack,
just this pounding shrillness, intense as the blare

of the light. The rioting of that claque
is demand to mate. As though it were rain,
one is sodden. Or, seething spear-points attack,

with rattlings. Most of the day you have lain
suffering ineptness — a full-length poultice
for sickness of spirit. The flight to Cockaigne

a chance, by late afternoon. Day's injustice
has all trees dazed as willows; but you make
the sea, in a light-struck car. It's featureless

there; the edge of grey water's laid, opaque
with light, sealed as the lip of an omelette,
on shore. Within it, like leaves that a rake

is rolling, like heavy edging of a net,
sea-wrack — which is, by thousands, the cicada.
Vaguely opaline, fabrics of the sunset;

nearby, dead panes of a yacht; in leather,
the wings that flit; coils of brown smoke, as though
away across there a city were on fire;

and these insects, once green, shown in fiasco:
they're stubbed-out, washed-up, become sodden brown.
A draggled hem. From frenzy, such overthrow;

how is a mystery. 'Not even the sun
will overstep its mark,' said Heraclitus.
That each element makes recompense was known

to Anaximander; 'for the injustice
they do, according to the ordinance
of Time.' Where the road of excess leads us

is this mess. (I have never sought guidance
of beefy, self-deluding William Blake.)
I see them abased with no exultance,

whose own complaint oversteps the mark. I walk
on rippled sand, the fallen wing of the shore,
in weird quietness. The water, engorged snake,

sluggishly winds. That sting like sweat's no more
in my head, but harmless rustlings. And these
free lines, these loose streamers, which the waves draw,

make me recall runnels sluicing glass; the ease
of another season. Ploughed fields under rain,
and like Epicurus's garden, the trees

rising quietly as mist, in me, in the pane,
from deep loam, where furrows end. In reverie
I see, too, how the shape of a human

is a hive for tears. Stiff or sinuously,
those roots of stumps, piled up, are warriors'
spokes, harness, ribands — all the stridency

of the mischievous and blood-coated creatures,
bogged, brought to grief. There is, if only we knew,
a land often kinder than ours, our failures'.

Twilight

These long stars
on

stalks
that have grown up

early
and are like

water
plants and that stand

in all
the pools and the lake

even
at the brim

of
the dark cup

before
your mouth these are

the one
slit star

Index